The last enemy that shall be destroyed is death.
(R.S.V. King James Edition: 1 Corinthians 15:26)

Skyraider 04 Down

Dieter Dengler

The Man The Ship The Plane

Skyraider 04 Down

Dieter Dengler

The Man The Ship The Plane

Charles. E. Mac Kay

Published by A Mackay (Publisher) Ltd for Nerton Publishing 2024
Copyright: C. E. Mac Kay ISBN: 9781838056773
Editor: C Barrowman   Layout and setting: R. Barrowman
Graphics and restoration: GM   Research: Morrison/Mac Kay

Printed and bound in Great Britain for A. MacKay (Publisher) Ltd.
Set in Times New Roman 16 point A4 by the publisher and printed in
A5 by Merchant City Print, High Street, Glasgow, North Britain

CONTENTS

Lieutenant (jg) Dieter Dengler, after rescue, at San Diego September 1966 at a press conference. "Man, it's great to be alive and free."

1

Foreword

The major part of this research was completed at the Mitchell Library Glasgow through Pro-Quest. Research was completed after one month using the Library of Congress, Trove.au, NARA, the United States National Archive Catalogue etc. Little Dieter needs to fly/Flucht aus Laos (German title), directed by Werner Herzog 1997, provided an excellent guideline. Later Herzog directed Christian Bale in the film Rescue Dawn 2006, Bale played Dieter Dengler the captured U.S. Navy officer. Sometimes when listening to the documentary it's difficult to differentiate who is talking, is it Dieter or is it Werner?

During the 1960s the BBC had a popular evening news programme - 24 Hours. Every night we would watch Julian Pettifer report on the campaign of Vietnam. We were treated to My Lai, Napalm, the naked girl running after a bombing attack, Tet, Linebaker, Yankee Station, Agent Orange, Rolling Thunder, aeroplanes bombing and diving. One episode showed a reporter flying in the back seat of a T-28D ground attack bomber - he was live reporting to the United States, his involvement in the bomber taking the Vietnam experience right into American homes. Reporting was everywhere making it *"The War"* in America. The war ended and its echoes roll on to this day.

South Vietnamese T-28D over Vietnam. The type used for the CBS broadcast

Earlier in 1945 the Royal Air Force pioneered air/jungle rescue by operating Beaufighters over the jungles of Malaya. This was extended to other areas of South East Asia Command, S.E.A.C. in 1946. This task was taken over by 81 Squadron (Thunderbolts) when 27 Squadron was disbanded. To improve the rescue service over sea and jungle five Lancasters were sent to re-equip 1348 Flight. The blue Lancasters well equipped and versatile inspired confidence among the British aircrews.

Avro Lancaster, it was this type of aircraft used in SEAC for jungle rescue

Dieter Dengler was a casualty of the Vietnam War, his recovery from the ordeal became an inspiration for others. Initially he was debriefed at Da Nang in South Vietnam by the Air Force. Then he was snatched by the Navy and returned to the carrier vessel USS *Ranger.* He was then de-briefed by the Navy at San Diego. Present were the men in smooth suits, shiny shoes, manicured nails and trim haircuts - the Central Intelligence Agency. The CIA found it difficult to believe him though they made no positive comment about his statements; the CIA de-classified archive was a ready source of information.

War and strife are difficult to talk about, difficult to recall. Even seeing human cruelty is just as hard and just as difficult to speak about. How can people do this? How can they behave like that? Why did Dieter survive? In Scripture in Saint John's Gospel John 2-25,

where Christ throws the buyers and sellers from the Temple it says:-
"...and did not need anyone to testify about human nature. He himself understood it well." This gives an early record, understanding and insight into human beings.

The Nuremberg Military Tribunals, after the Second World War charged defendants with crimes against humanity in all twelve trials. Those crimes were enumerated in Article II(1)(c) of Law No. 10: *Atrocities and offenses, including but not limited to murder, extermination, enslavement, deportation, imprisonment, torture, rape, or other inhumane acts committed against any civilian population, or persecutions on political, racial or religious grounds whether or not in violation of the domestic laws of the country where perpetrated.* What happened to Dieter Dengler was a crime against humanity these were crimes against Dieter Dengler and the others.

Publisher's Note: The views, conclusions and presentation in this publication are those of the author and researcher and not of any official body.

The Researchers   *25 May 2024*

Netherton

2

Dieter Dengler

Dieter Dengler was born in Wildberg, Wurttemberg, the Black Forest, Germany, on 22 May 1938. His childhood and early life were full of hardships. Surviving under Allied bombing and surviving under Allied occupation gave him a survivor's instinct. Later in military service, he was trained in escape, evasion and survival at the navy SERE survival school where he was the only student to gain weight. Dieter never completed the course, because he kept on escaping. He escaped twice from the entire naval installation. Once, he called in to the Shore Patrol to pick him up at a saloon, where he was enjoying a burger and a beer, having escaped by avoiding his guard and commandeering his uniform, then sauntering out the gate. He had in his possession a letter of commendation from the Secretary of the Navy, acknowledging this feat. Dieter was also inspired by his maternal grandfather, Hermann Schnuerle, who was subjected to public humiliation and was sentenced to work in the rock mine for a year for refusing to vote for Adolf Hitler. Growing up in extreme poverty, he and his brothers used to collect wallpaper from bombed-out buildings to extract the nutrients left in the wallpaper paste and also scavenged the nearby French Army Moroccan camp for leftover food. He also scavenged for scrap and had built a bicycle for himself becoming the first in the town to own one. At the age of 14, he started working as an apprentice, working six days a week building giant clocks and clock faces to repair German cathedrals. Despite the fact that he was regularly beaten by the other boys and the blacksmith was harsh and strict, he thanked him later for teaching him to be "tough enough to survive". As a boy, he had determined to become a pilot after witnessing an American fighter plane firing its guns and flying very close to the window he was watching from.

After he saw an advertisement for pilots in an American magazine, he again commenced salvaging scrap metal to sell, and completed his apprenticeship at 18, (Dieter Dengler was an apprentice

Wildberg in the Black Forest

B-24 and B-17s with P-47 escort over the Reich

P-51D Mustang used for ground attack over Germany

at Uhrenfabrik Perrot, who made tower clocks in Germany from 1954 to 1957.) He wanted to join the airline Lufthansa but he did not have the educational qualifications. Dieter joined the United States Air Force 7 June 1957, number AF12531162. Despite being promised pilot training, he was assigned to the motor pool as a mechanic after completing the basic training he later got an assignment as an armament technician.

Earlier he had entered the United States at New York on 14 May 1957 on the liner SS *America*. At the time the SS *America's* route was New York-LeHavre-Bremerhaven-Cobh. Dieter's passport was issued near the place of his birth, the town of Calw, in the German Federal Republic (West Germany), on 17 July 1956. On 24 August 1964 his passport was extended to 14 January 1968 and signed and stamped by the burgomaster but this time at Stuttgart. On Dengler's naturalization documents (No.19192) he was described as being 5ft 9in in height, with brown eyes and brown hair, weighing 155 pounds. At the time of his application for naturalization he was serving at Lackland Air Force Base, San Antonio, Texas. He served in the Air Force from 1957 to 1961 becoming a naturalised citizen on 3 August 1960. He did not achieve flight status because the Air Force required graduates for aircrew. He left the Air Force and then worked with his brother at a bakery shop near San Francisco for some time and then enrolled into San Francisco City College but later transferred to the College of San Mateo to study aeronautics in 1962. His handle at college was *Die Katze* (his nickname to his German friends - "the Cat"). College of San Mateo was one of few places in California where anyone could go to ground school for free. San Mateo Junior College, as it was then known, launched its aeronautics programme

SS AMERICA

Beech T-34 Mentor

North American T-28B
U.S. Navy Trainer

Douglas Skyraider

during the Depression to supply engineers, technicians and crew to the new San Francisco International Airport. When he started his course Dieter Dengler was still desperately poor, living in a Volkswagen van that he kept running with parts he stole in the dead of night from other vehicles on the street. In the van he kept boxes of dirt, in which he grew vegetables for food. But he was tall, handsome and charismatic and he studied hard, becoming Aeronautics Student of the Semester in 1962 and graduating in January 1963. He passed the Navy's aviation cadet exam soon after. Upon graduation, he successfully applied for the US Navy aviation cadet program, completed his flight training Pensacola Naval Air Station on the T-34 and T-28 and trained as an attack pilot on the Douglas AD Skyraider at the Naval Air Station Corpus Christi, Texas.

Dengler is a common name throughout Germany, Austria, Switzerland, Hungary and Belgium. In Germany the Dengler's are widely scattered but the main groupings appear to be in southern Germany: Bavaria, Baden, Wurttemberg and Austria. Dengler was the name for a farmer or a dealer in Spelt, which is a kind of wheat. Spelt, which is a derivative of the Old Germanic word Dinkel, was a grain like barley and wheat which was grown extensively in the German speaking states during the Middle Ages; Spelt was sold as a cereal crop and formed a large part of the diet at this time. Dieter's father, Reinhold Dengler, a *Wehrmacht Feldwebel,* was killed during the Second World War on the Russian Front at Kiev during the summer

GM/USNAVY

CVA-61 USS Ranger

of 1943. Dieter was accompanied to New York on the *America* by his brother Martin, who was the baker, his other brother Klaus remained in Germany with his mother. Martin ultimately lived in Pacifica, California. Klaus, a forestry official, lived on the edge of the Black Forest in Southern Germany.

Dieter Dengler was posted to VA-145 squadron while it was on shore duty at Naval Air Station Alameda, California and in 1965 he joined the carrier USS *Ranger* with his squadron to sail for the coast of Vietnam. The United States had resumed the bombing of Communist North Vietnam after a 37-day lull, during which President Johnson's *"peace offensive"* was launched and failed .On Tuesday, 1 February 1966 a Skyhawk from *Ranger* crashed into the sea. *Ranger* had commenced flight operations that day at 08.12. (*Ranger* completed flight operations that day at 22.26). That day Lt (jg) Dieter Dengler was on his first combat mission, as the last of a four plane flight, he was flying a combat mission over Laos, though he had flown about 20 missions off the USS *Ranger* at "Dixie Station," into South Vietnam. *Ranger* had commenced Seventh Fleet operations on Dixie Station from 15-20 January 1966.

Dixie Station was a carrier staging area about 100 miles southeast of Cam Ranh Bay at 11° N and 110° E and was off the Mekong Delta to the south. The setup of Dixie Station meant that four aircraft

South China Sea area of operations - Dixie and Yankee Stations

carriers were deployed to the combat theatre; one would operate from Dixie Station and two from Yankee Station, with the fourth carrier at the Subic Bay Naval Base in the Philippines for the rest and recuperation of her sailors and Marines and for maintenance of the carrier. The carrier squadrons on Dixie Station destroyed numerous enemy ammunition dumps, fortified positions, and storage huts in the jungles of Vietnam. The air wing aviators from the Dixie Station carrier familiarized themselves with combat operations in the less lethal skies of South Vietnam before they were deployed to Yankee Station off North Vietnam. Yankee Station was the point from which the Navy launched its Rolling Thunder missions and commenced in the offshore waters south of the Demilitarized Zone prior to April 1966 and thereafter to the north of the waters in the Demilitarized Zone. With Air Force and Marine airfields in South Vietnam largely completed and operating combat aircraft by August 1966, the Navy disestablished Dixie Station.

That last day on the aircraft carrier Dieter took with him a combination of personal gear and normal escape and evasion survival equipment. This included a compass on his watchband, a .38 pistol, a fishing line and extra hooks, a mirror, high protein foodstuffs such as raisins, salted nuts and pepperoni, extra clothing and a green waterproof nylon sleeping bag. Dengler was in the four plane formation flying in poor visibility as part of an interdiction mission near Mu Gia Pass between Laos and North Vietnam. His call-sign was, *"Skyraider 04."* As the flight neared their assigned target, an anti-aircraft battery at a road intersection, they received a distress call from a flight of VA-115 "Spads" (Skyraiders) off USS *Kitty Hawk* (CVA-64). A pilot from VA-115 had been downed by anti-aircraft fire and Lt. jg Dengler and his fellow pilots of VA-145 were to provide protective cover until search and rescue (SAR) forces could arrive. The pilots of VA-145 dropped their ordnance on target and flew towards the downed aircraft from VA-115 then Lt. jg Dengler failed to report off target. Radio contact could not be established with him and while SAR procedures had immediately been implemented, no sign of Lt. jg. Dengler was found.

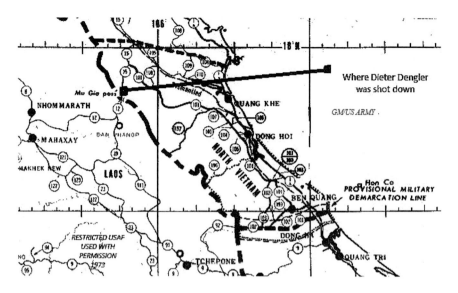

Area in Vietnam-Laos where Dieter Dengler was shot down

It was not until the second day of search and rescue that his crashed Skyraider was spotted. The starboard wing had been blown off by a 57mm shell. Another burst had hit his engine but he managed to bomb his target and take out the anti-aircraft battery which had hit him. As the Skyraider came out of its bombing run Dengler knew he was going to crash. He could not control the aircraft and the only clearing he could see was less than 300 feet long. Surrounding the clearing were trees about 150 feet high and 3 feet thick. The Skyraider shuddered and hit a tree and the port wing sheared off; the plane veered wildly and what was left of the starboard wing hit another tree, the tail came off. The fuselage then flipped over two or three times. Dieter took the crash position and placed his hands in front of his face and was knocked unconscious during the crash.

When he came to he remembered struggling to open the jammed canopy and then being on his back about 100 yards from the Douglas Skyraider - a plume of smoke rising into the sky - his first thought was escape! He was wearing his heavy green flight suit and a nylon sleeping bag taped to his back. Unfortunately for Lt Dengler, no one at the time knew that he had crashed. A few minutes later, the other

20

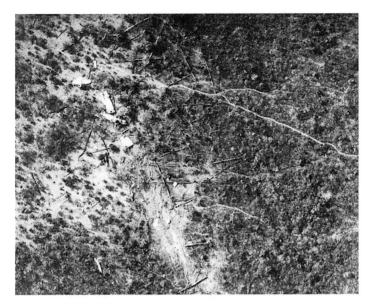

2 February 1966, Dieter Dengler's crashed Skyraider, wreckage top left hand corner showing fuselage, tail, wings and engine, later Dieter and his wife found the engine

members of his flight realized that he was missing. They began a route search, on the reverse course they had flown inbound, but could not find him. An HU-16 began a monitoring guard for a beeper signal. None was heard. The next day, USS *Ranger* launched four A-1 Skyraiders to accomplish second route search. This time they located the wreckage. Helicopters from Udorn RTAFB scrambled to the scene. Without radio contact, the rescue force was not supposed to attempt SAR.

A helicopter did attempt a rescue and hovered directly over the crash site, the rescue crew could see that the cockpit was empty. With no rescue objective, they left the area. Everyone flying overhead hoped he was still alive and evading somewhere in the jungle. Dengler, his helmet ripped off, head gashed with a cut behind the ear and left leg badly bruised, had scrambled out of the wreckage and

United States Air Force 1966

*Grumman HU-16 albatross used for air sea rescue and
Communication platform*

made for a nearby river. He saw the rescue attempt and tried to raise them on his radio which did not work. He heard shouting so he buried his survival gear, radio, and pistol and moved off to the north, believing that his trackers would search to the west, toward Thailand. But at noon the next day, 3 February, he was captured while trying to cross a trail. Dengler had been captured by Pathet Lao soldiers who were - pro-communist Laotians. They were mountain tribesmen dressed in American-style shirts and trousers, carrying American weapons and wearing sunglasses. One of them held a rifle to his head while another searched him. Then they tied his hands and hit him on the head a few times with their fists. They took away his watch, his compass and his personal papers. To prove his German accent he carried his expired German passport. He was frog marched through the jungle for six hours. Local people guided his captors from one village to the next. Each was dressed differently. None wore military rank. None spoke English. At night they drove four big stakes into the ground and he was spread-eagled between them. He spent the night trying to scare away the mosquitoes and then the leeches came crawling up his legs. By morning, he was a mass of insect stings and mosquito and leech bites. Once, he was tied to a tree while his Pathet Lao captors fired away trying to see how close they could come to hit him. This was termed *"Laotian Roulette."* As they moved along the trail they occasionally stopped at small villages and the men, women, and children came out of their huts and clustered about them. The huts were called "bashas". It was a hut of four walls, with a leaf roof; they were very hot with a lot of mosquitoes, leeches crawling in and green snakes (Bamboo Vipers). A week passed before the party stopped at a village which Dieter Dengler remembered as Yamalot (or Yommalath District). He noticed that the villagers were not happy with the soldiers who took provisions from the villagers, leaving them with virtually nothing. He also noted that the villagers lived in the jungle and only returned to the huts at night to eat and sleep. They continually asked the soldiers when would the war be over and when they could return to their fields. All that existed for the Villagers was Laos, Cambodia and Vietnam: for them the world outside did not exist.

On the 2 February, the European Command of the U. S. Navy in Frankfurt (Main) received the order to inform the next of kin of the missing pilot Dieter Dengler. Dressed in civilian clothes Captain William N. Hatch drove his car to Calw. At the door of the house at Metzgergasse 22, he rang an old fashioned door bell. A woman opened the door, her grey hair was combed straight back. Captain Hatch asked her: *"Are you Mrs. Dengler?"* Eying him suspiciously she nodded, then conducted him to her living room. Then he told her gently that her son was missing over North Vietnam. Hatch expected a flood of tears but Mrs Dengler stood erect and said, *"I believe in the Lord, He does not make any mistakes, therefore I do not worry about my Dieter. I have no fear."* Four weeks later he returned with still no news for Mrs Dengler concerning her son. He returned on 28 June with the same sad news.

One of the company a Laotian officer could speak French. He told Dengler he had been four times to the Geneva Conference. At first he was friendly and taking out a camera he took a picture of Dieter. He said he wanted to send the photo to Dengler's family along with a letter stating the captured pilot was safe. He gave Dengler paper to write to his fiancée and his mother. Dengler printed letters to both, using the entire paper. He was held in a huge cave and for nearly a week Dengler had been eating nothing but rice. The officer gave him some sugar and a couple of eggs and he told Dengler that he could write some more letters. He then pulled out another piece of paper and asked him to sign his name. It was typed and phrased in perfect English and it said that the Americans were dropping bombs on innocent women and children and that as an American officer he was personally opposed to this policy and being forced to fly on these missions by the U.S. government. Dieter Dengler would not sign that paper. The Laotian officer then said something to the guards who beat him on the head with bamboo sticks, then pummelled his face and ears with their fists. Next morning, the officer approached again to sign the paper - Dengler refused. The officer ordered the guards to bring a water buffalo to the mouth the cave. The guards tied his hands and then his feet and they ran a rope 15 or 20 feet long to the buffalo's collar. Laughing, they prodded the animal until it trotted. Dengler was dragged headfirst over sharp roots sticking out of the trail.

His uniform was tattered; the skin on his legs was shredded and he bled profusely. More beatings followed, but on the tenth day of his capture, Dengler was taken from Yamalot with the statement still unsigned.

He and two guards walked to another village, where they spent the night. About midnight, Dengler took advantage of the guards' heavy sleeping to escape. He found his shoes, walked to the lowest spot around a riverbed then followed the stream for two hours, unfortunately returning almost to the place from which he started out. He had walked in a circle. At dawn, he began climbing a karst mountain, reaching its peak about noon. (A karst mountain is made of limestone – a sedimentary rock composed mainly of shells or skeletons of marine organisms such as corals and molluscs and microscopic marine creatures.) He signalled two passing U.S. F-105 Thunderchiefs, one of which dipped a wing and circled. But no rescue came and Dengler, exhausted, sick from poisonous fruit he had eaten and cut from the sharp karst ridges, climbed back down the mountain, using vines to control his descent. Near the bottom, drained from

GM/UNITED STATES AIR FORCE

Republic F-105D Thunderchief - the "Thud"

fatigue, he collapsed into a waterhole. Moments later he was quickly surrounded by a platoon of Pathet Lao, who dragged him out of the waterhole and bound him tightly, cutting the circulation in both of his arms. As one Laotian tried to club Dengler with a rifle butt, the rifle went off and fired a bullet through the stomach of a comrade, killing him instantly. A third soldier shot the first through both legs before order was restored. Then they beat Dengler and pushed an ant nest over his head. Though in great torment, he was lucky to be alive. Then he was handed over to the Vietnamese, they believed the Laotians could not handle, *"...the bad American."* The Vietnamese took over as Dengler's guards but then handed him back to the Pathet Lao in a stockade deep in the jungle.

One night, the guards stuffed him upright into a hole with at least five of them keeping a close watch. At dawn they travelled on, past a North Vietnamese training camp, new buildings and a new roadway, reaching Houei Het and Par Kung three days later, on the afternoon of Valentine's Day. They reached the prison camp, a collection of bamboo huts sitting on stilts about four feet off the ground. They pushed Dieter into the darkness of one the huts. They put handcuffs on his wrists and stuck his feet into wooden blocks that weighed about 30 or 40 pounds. From his hut Dengler saw six other prisoners across in another hut a few feet away. Several of them were in bad

Vietnamese bamboo hut

Bamboo fence and ditch surrounding a Vietnamese village

Bamboo hut used by the Viet Cong for training purposes

A Viet Cong cave of the type Dieter Dengler was imprisoned in heavily fortified and strengthened against attack

shape covered with big sores on their bodies. One of them called back and that his name was Duane Martin; he was an Air Force lieutenant, a helicopter pilot, who he had been captured nine months earlier. Some of the other prisoners had been there more than two years. Lt Martin had been aboard an HH-43B with Capt. Tom Curtis (pilot) SSgt William Robinson and Airman Arthur Black. All of these men had been shot down during an attempted rescue in September 1965. Captain Curtis, Sgt Robinson and AIC Black were interred in the Hanoi prison system then the North Vietnamese released these three men in 1973.

As they waited, conditions worsened at the prison. Guards gave them a small rice ration that they supplemented by killing and eating snakes and rats. Once they caught a snake that had eaten two rats, they ate the rats as well. Once a day the guards allowed them out to dump their toilet pails but most of the time they were locked in wooden foot stocks and tied or handcuffed. The trip to empty the pail was dangerous because the guards were very cruel. Sometimes they shot at a prisoner if he moved too slowly or too fast. At one point they witnessed an Air Force Lieutenant, who had tried to escape, being beheaded. The men feared being shot if they stumbled or fell. After ten days, they were moved to a new location and a jungle camp where food was even scarcer. The anticipated rains never came. By

June the men overheard guards talking about killing them so there would be fewer alive to eat the precious rations. The drought meant no more drinking water and no baths. The prisoners were covered with lice, infestations and full of infection.

Over time the guards were given nicknames, Little Hitler, Crazy Horse (who looked like a horse), Sot, Dam and Windy etc. but Little Hitler was the worst. Dieter recalled, "*... he was short - about 5 feet 2 inches - and he wore a blue and - yellow loincloth. He had dark skin, little squirrelly eyes and a big belly. He always carried a submachine gun. He did his best to torment us and he succeeded lots of times. He knew, for example, that we wanted water desperately, so he'd bring some in a pot and place it just out of our reach. Then he'd pour the water on the ground and laugh. Another of his tricks was to stand one of us in foot blocks outside the hut and take the man's handcuffs off. Then he'd tell the other guards that the prisoner refused to wear handcuffs and should be punished. Right away they'd beat him and fire bullets at his feet.*" Then there was Jumbo, fat and dreamy faced and didn't care about anything. After about eight days they were marched to another camp - Crazy Horse declaring they were marching to freedom - but this camp was just like the last one.

In the morning the routine was wake up with the chickens, rub bamboo together to make a fire, at about nine breakfast, which was rice, they were allowed to eat at a table but after a few minutes the guards would shout at them and push them back into the hut. During the day, the heat was so unbearable that the guards when not on duty simply went to sleep: in mid-afternoon they'd wake up, go out to check their traps for animals and look for edible leaves and bark, around five they'd let the prisoners out again for another ten minute meal before putting them back in foot blocks for the rest of the night.
The most nerve-racking part of the prisoner's routine was the singing. Every night the guards would sing the same propaganda songs, over and over again. Occasionally the guards would push them out of their huts and hang them upside down from trees or fire shots at their feet as they moved about.

The prisoner's developed their own routine. Firstly they would sing songs that they all knew. Then on a Sunday they would set aside time for worship, they had no Bible but they would discuss the scriptures and the being of God the Higher Power. Finally they would close their simple worship with prayer - then there was nothing more to do than sit around for the rest of the time.

The prisoner's diet was rice - just rice. Then, about a month after they had moved to the new camp in March, the food supply suddenly stopped. Once every four or five days the guards would go and check their traps. If something had been caught, it probably would have been dead for a number of days; other animals had scavenged the carcass in the trap leaving little to eat. For some reason, when they caught a pig, the guards would stick the raw meat into a bamboo container and let it rot there for several days. Maggots would crawl all over it, and it would stink so bad that the guards would hold their noses. Most of the prisoners were already used to eating the remains. Dengler thought they had lost their senses at first, but after a while it didn't bother him either. At mealtime, they'd take turns dipping coconut shells into a pot of cold food brought by a guard. If they had meat, they cut it up first to make sure that each of them got his fair share. One afternoon they found a frog under the floor of the hut. They divided it, raw, among the seven prisoners, Dengler got its heart. The heart was smaller than a watch case, but at least it was food. At night the rats came in. They caught them in traps baited with rice. The rats made very good eating. They would cook them to the extent of searing off their fur, then eat the head, legs, tail, skin - everything. The snakes that were caught were small, but most of them had rats in their stomachs. For the prisoners this was a double feast.

They never received any medical attention and any medical work that was to be carried out was very primitive. Teeth were removed with a nail and the broken pieces torn from the gum: stomach disorders were common, partially cured by eating charcoal. Ants and bugs were everywhere in the hut making life more intolerable.

From the start of captivity, they all talked of escape. They decided to wait for the rains which would begin in May. One of the prisoners made a crude calendar and scratched off the days with a piece of charcoal. D-Day was to be Dieter Dengler's birthday - May 22. The escape plan gave them hope and kept them alive. Chiu and Martin

*Air America
Curtiss C-46*

were the sickest. In the escape plan, Chiu was to go with DeBruin (who had been shot down in a C-46, 5 September 1963) and Martin with Dengler so each would have the best possible chance. Thanee, Promsuwan, and Indradat arranged to go together. The plan was a good one. They carefully studied the guards for a week, tracing every move, always noting where the weapons were kept. Knowing it was a three-hour hike to the village at Par Kung and that few Laotians would be in the area after dark, they planned to slip out during the guards' supper, seize the weapons, kill the guards, then set up signal fires for a C-130 that passed over every night. With luck, they hoped to be rescued in the morning.

In March, they started hiding rice in bamboo containers. They picked up empty ammunition clips that the guards had thrown away and stored them inside their huts. Making fire they rubbed dry bamboo together and heated the clips until they were soft and pliable, then they pounded the clips with rocks into little knives. Dengler tore up part of his sleeping bag to make a rucksack; another prisoner made a rucksack out of his shorts. By April they had perfected a technique to get out of the handcuffs. The prisoner who had made the calendar kept crossing off the days.

The rains didn't come in May: the rice supply was almost gone, the guards caught fewer and fewer animals in their traps and they were hungry too. In June they learned that Little Hitler had told the other guards that if they shot the prisoners in the back and dragged their bodies into the bush they'd have all the food to themselves. The prisoners could not afford to wait for the rains. Their only chance of survival was to break out right away and try to make air contact. They were now let out of the huts once a week to go to the latrine.

Physically their muscles were so stiff that they could hardly walk. If they delayed the escape much longer they'd be far too weak to break out.

Each afternoon about five in the afternoon, the guards would walk to the kitchen, pick up their food in turtle shells and then walk back to their hut. The prisoners thought of breaking through the floor of their hut and make their way to the guard's hut to snatch a rifle. They estimated it would take two minutes and seven seconds. The food supply was now so critical that five of the guards left the camp and went to get rice in a village a few miles away. Only ten guards remained.

When the guards went to eat on the night of 29 June Dengler loosened his bindings and crawling under a fence through a hole he had dug out earlier he crept underneath their hut, he managed to reach the weapons hut. Dieter Dengler had edged past the logs and dashed across the open space. As soon as he reached the porch the other prisoners started coming through the hole. Dengler grabbed two M-ls, a carbine, and a couple of Chinese rifles. He loaded them quickly and passed them out to the other prisoners and turned to face the kitchen. Two minutes and seven seconds – exactly as had been predicted but just as he began passing rifles to Martin and Indradat the guards discovered their escape.

All of a sudden, firing, the guards were running out of their hut towards the prisoners firing as they went, the bullets flying by their heads. They yelled, "ute, ute," stop, stop, stop, to the guards, then returned fire. Seven guards fell dead in their tracks. Three of them fled into the jungle. Thankfully none of them had been wounded in the exchange of fire; still, they were in trouble. They knew that there was a village only a mile or so from the camp. If these three guards had gone to get help, search parties would be after them in half an hour. The prisoners had rifles and machetes. One prisoner went back to the hut to get their signalling devices, rucksacks, and food. Five minutes later they were moving out on the trail. Air Force Capt. Duane W. Martin and Dieter Dengler knelt down to pray. *"Dear God, please let us get home. Help us now because we just can't do it by ourselves."* Then two of the prisoners broke away and headed east never to be seen again. The other five prisoners, including Dengler and Martin, walked south to the closest ridge, feet swollen and bleeding.

They spent the night near a river, which varied, sometimes it was 10 feet wide, and coming into a lower part, it became 100, 200 feet wide. It rained and leeches swarmed all over their bodies, too exhausted to care. They got up again at dawn and decided to split into groups of two and three. Duane Martin and Dieter Dengler decided to stay together. They split the ammunition, the others taking 24 rounds of ammunition in return for one of their machetes. Then they shook hands and wished each other luck.

They had no idea where they were so they decided to follow the river. It was rising now because of the rain, in some places it was only five feet wide; in others more than 100 feet wide and very deep. On the third or fourth day, they decided to build a raft of banana trees. It took them eight hours: but then they found another raft which they floated along for several hundred yards. Then they heard a waterfall. They jumped and swam as fast as they could to the shore. They hit a night fisherman, standing in the water fishing for trout; the trout were near the waterfall. The fisherman shouted then they hit him. The raft swept over the falls and was smashed. He went one way and the two escaped prisoners went the other. They still had their machete but they didn't dare to cut a trail. If they couldn't go straight through a section of jungle, they'd go around it or try to bend the bush or crawl under it on their stomachs. Dengler's arms were numb and the skin had been ripped from his feet and legs exposing the bone.

Both of them were now very weak and kept passing out (lack of food). At night to keep warm they would wrap their arms around each other and hug. They realized now that they might not make it. Dieter promised Duane that if he ever got out he'd visit his wife and family. Duane Martin said he'd do the same for him. Then Duane got malaria; his fever was very high and he couldn't walk and finally they came to a deserted village. Dieter laid him in a hammock; they were too weak to walk. Dieter had contracted Jaundice. Their food supply was almost gone and their clothes were in shreds. They didn't have the strength to carry their weapons and ammunition so they discarded them in the bush. Next morning on the fourteenth day of their escape -

leaving Duane Martin in his hammock Dieter went back into the bush to search for the ammunition they had discarded. He slept in the woods that night and then crawled back to the village. Duane was still there. And to them this was the greatest thing. Duane laughed and Dieter laughed and they hugged each other. Duane was so happy that Dieter found three rounds of ammunition and Dieter was so happy that he was still alive. They broke the tips off the bullets, poured out the powder and rubbed the bamboo sticks together – *Pffft* - at last they had fire. They boiled some leaves and tapioca; it was the first hot meal they'd had in many months and it really cheered them up.

They kept the fire going then they tied some rags to bamboo sticks for signalling. Later that night they heard a plane. It circled over the village and dropped a couple of parachute flares. *"Hey, he saw us,"* Duane cried. *"He's gonna get us in the morning."* They stayed awake all night talking about what they'd eat tomorrow. The plane never came back. They waited all that day before giving up. At dawn next morning - the seventeenth day after their escape - they stumbled away from the village. Suddenly, a black-haired man in a loincloth started running toward them. He carried a long machete - curved at the end. *"Amerikali, Amerikali,"* he yelled. They nodded their heads and mumbled, *"Sentai, Sentai"* ("hello, hello"). But the man kept running. Dieter fell back and tried to stand up. The machete was already moving through the air thud thud thud - the first blow hit Duane on the leg; the second cut into his shoulder just below the neck. Duane screamed and Dieter threw up his hands as if to say *"No."* he knew Duane was dead. He couldn't grasp the situation; he just stood there with his mouth wide open. Then the man swung at him. The tip of his machete missed his throat by half an inch. Not knowing where he got the strength Dieter moved and started to run. He turned around and ran and ran hit into the jungle and ran up a gully - his legs didn't hurt anymore.

That night Dieter Dengler crawled back to the village forced to eat raw snales to survive. He thought it was his village and he wanted to burn it down. He was angry and the balance of his mind had gone. He sat in front of a fire and threw everything on it. He didn't care if he was caught. Then he heard a sound, a plane a C-130. It circled over

the village and dropped about twenty parachute flares. Next morning he waited and waited but the aircraft did not return. *"God,"* he said. *"What's the matter with those guys?"* He knew they wouldn't save him now. He picked up one of the parachutes and tore the panels out. That afternoon, he crawled up to a nearby ridge. He saw a little hut there and he said, *"That's where I'm going to die."* Dieter Dengler prayed. *"God, forgive me for the bad things I've done in life. I just can't fight it anymore. Please let me die. I don't want to wake up."*
But he did wake up. He was really thirsty and he said, *"To hell with it. Those guys aren't gonna lick me."*

Dieter stuffed the parachute panels into his rucksack and fell down the ridge losing more skin off his feet, he could feel no pain. His mind was flooded with earlier peaceful days, deep-sea fishing, skiing, building a chalet, buying a Porsche. His hopes and dreams were dashed and he thought back to Lakeland Air Force Base where he threw away a piece of bread: he vowed never to do that again.

He needed food badly and the searchers, whenever they ate, left bits of food behind - rice, peppers, fish heads and bones. His luck held for four more days. At a fork in the stream, he struck out away from the search party just before he began fading in and out of consciousness and suffering daily periods of hallucination, often imagining that he and Martin were talking. He could easily have given himself away. He ate snails and leaves, slept under a log one night, on top of a rock next to a waterfall. He suffered intense pain in his kidneys and coughed blood. Whenever he rested, he needed two hours just to arise and prepare to move again. Then he was followed through the forest by a bear that was waiting for him and strangely like a silent sentinel he called this symbol of death his only friend.

On his 22nd day of freedom - he took the parachute panels out of the rucksack and tied them end to end trying to lay out an "SOS" by the river. The job taking him two hours, then he wrapped another panel around a bamboo slick. Then he passed out again. He was down in a little gully. There was a wall going up sharply and there was only 200 feet of space for a pilot to see him. He was awakened by an approaching aeroplane an A-1 Skyraider flown by Lieutenant Colonel

A-1H Skyraider "Sandy"52-139738 of the 1st SOS

Eugene P. Deatrick. Dieter gathered all his remaining strength, started waving the bamboo stick and then - zoom - the plane was past and gone. He waved and jumped again and then there were two A-1s of Air Force Skyraiders from the 1st Air Commando Squadron which Dietrick had been in command of for four months, controlled by a Lockheed EC-121 aircraft.

The flight had departed from its original schedule over the jungle but technical difficulties with the aircraft had meant a change of plan. The Skyraiders saw him. Deatrick contacted the EC-121for advice to continue with the operation. One Skyraider stayed low, the other climbed higher for radio transmission. Had the first plane not been in a bank at exactly the correct spot, the pilot would never have seen Dengler because of the A-1s broad cowling and low wings which made downward visibility poor. Had he flown 20 yards to the right or left, he would not have seen him because the jungle would have obscured his view. But the aircraft turned and came back several times, waggling its wings. Dieter was so happy that he started crying and shouting and rolling around on his back - then he collapsed.

All of a sudden, around 11.00, Dieter heard the sound of a helicopter, a Sikorsky Jolly Green Giant, which appeared 200 feet above his head. A steel rope began descending slowly towards him

Lockheed EC-121

Sikorsky HH3-E Jolly Green Giant

Jolly Green Giant refuelled by a Hercules

USNAVY/LOC/GM

Helicopter rescue of LCDR Thomas Tucker who was lifted from deep within Haiphong Harbour 31 AUG 66 using a cable system similar to Dieter Dengler's rescue

and there was the rescue harness; a slender device with three little arms folded into its side. Before the helicopter had arrived he heard shooting from the Viet Cong. Dieter grabbed the rope and had to press the arms down to make a seat but he couldn't unzip the plastic cover. He clawed at the harness and finally wrenched one arm free and gave a little signal, then he was hanging sideways; he didn't know if he could hold on much longer. Dieter said, *"God, don't let a bullet hit me now; not after all this hell I've been through."* Then he saw an airman's leg and green trousers standing in the door. An American leg - he grabbed it and cried, *"I am going where you are going."* He did not let go until he landed at Da Nang.

The helicopter crew had reeled Dieter up and pulled him into the cabin. As SSgt W. Gladish pulled him inside, Dieter grabbed Air Force Medical Corpsman Leonard's leg and exclaimed *"Oh my God!"* Bill Gladish pulled the survivor away from Mike Leonard. Then they searched him for hidden explosives or a weapon. While they searched him they heard him yell that his name was Lt. Dieter Dengler. Over the roar of the rotors and jet engines Airman Leonard was unsure of

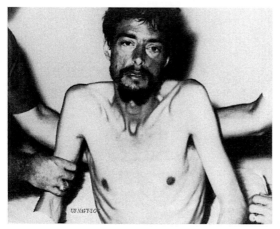

Dieter Dengler on the day of his rescue at Da Nang

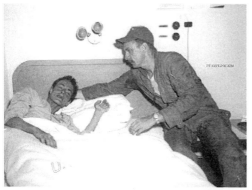

In the Admiral's cabin USS Ranger

Now in recovery Dieter with the pilots of VA-145 on the USS Ranger

what he had heard. As they crossed the area, the survivor again told them that he was Lt Dieter Dengler. Leonard told the pilot Captain William E. Cowell the name and the pilot radioed base with the information. On the flight Dengler lost consciousness with fits three times on the flight back to Da Nang but the crew managed to feed him pineapple juice and beans. They had stripped him down in case he was carrying explosives but all they found was a headless snake. No-one at base, in the helicopter, or the escort aircraft knew who Lt. Dieter Dengler was. Back at Da Nang AB they phoned 7th AF Headquarters at Saigon and told them they had a helicopter inbound to Da Nang AB with a Lieutenant Dieter Dengler on board.

The helicopter crew flying Dengler back to their base at Da Nang AB were ecstatic upon discovering they had rescued an escaped POW. Neither the crew nor Dengler could have been ready for the pandemonium that awaited them at Da Nang. As they taxied into their ramp, they could see a huge crowd waiting for them. Word had spread like a wildfire through Da Nang that the helicopter had picked up an escaped POW. Every senior officer and photographer on base was on hand, along with a large contingent of fighter pilots and rescue men. When he had been launched from his aircraft carrier six months earlier Dengler weighed 157 pounds. When he stepped from the Jolly Green Giant helicopter that had rescued him, he weighed only 90 pounds. Lt Dengler and every man greeting him knew that he was an exceptionally lucky pilot. On arriving at the hospital he couldn't move his arms, head or legs but he felt peace. Believing this to be a dream he thought: *"...this must be life after death."*

After three or four days at Da Nang hospital a small contingent of the Navy took Dengler from the Air Force station where he was to be debriefed. Dengler had been snatched by the Navy from the Air Force. He was returned to a celebration held in his honour aboard the USS *Ranger* shortly after 4pm on 21 July 1966. He was given the captain's cabin for rest and comfort but he could only find sleep in the cockpit of the A-1 Skyraider. On 25 July Dieter was flown to Clark Air Force Base, where he was taken onto a Lockheed C-141 Starlifter and flown to the United States. The next morning he arrived at Travis Air Force Base in northern California, where he had a brief reunion with Marina and his brother Martin. On 27 July, Dieter was admitted to Balboa Naval Hospital San Diego under the care of Doctor Allan Holmes, where he was to remain as a patient for more than two months. For his first few nights he found the bed too soft and he slept on the floor.

After Dengler's return, Air America searched the Houei Het region for DeBruin and Chiu but rescuers never found a sign of them. Rumours and unverified reports suggested that DeBruin had been recaptured but he was last officially accounted for in May 1966 (before the 29 June escape attempt), when a Pathet Lao representative mentioned his whereabouts to an American Embassy officer. His fate after June 1966, along with Chiu's, remains a mystery. What became of Thanee and Promsuwan also no one knows. Only Indradat besides Dengler of the original seven is known to have come out of Laos alive. Indradat, who parted with the other, Thais following the escape, was recaptured after a 33-day evasion and severely beaten but he held on to be rescued along with 50 other prisoners (none of them Americans) during a raid upon their camp in January 1967 - the most successful prison camp raid of the war. But between Dengler's escape in 1966 and the 1973 prisoner repatriation, no American POWs were returned from Laos. In September 1966 a press release reported that five prisoners had died in captivity, five others were released and many of the 303 Americans listed as Missing in Action were probably in Communist hands.

Communication and security problems began shortly after the rescue team deposited Dieter Dengler in a field hospital at Da Nang. Congressman Robert Taft of Ohio and two reporters, Richard Kirkpatrick of the Cincinnati Enquirer and Rod Williams of WSAI Radio in Cincinnati, happened to be in the receiving room. Unaware that the pilot had been shot down over Laos or that any revelation of his story might threaten diplomatic relations in the region; Kirkpatrick wrote an article on Taft's visit to the hospital that included a reference to recovery of an unidentified American pilot in North Vietnam near the Laotian border.

When contacted by the Military Assistance Command, Kirkpatrick and Williams readily agreed to withhold the story until the command issued a communique but Joseph Fried got word of what had happened and telephoned the MACV Office of Information for details. (Earlier, a reporter from Associated Press had obviously talked to a knowledgeable insider to get the story - Gene Dietrick, the unit commander and the pilot who had spotted Dengler. Later the reporter flew on a mission up north with the command.)

Joseph Fried knew the name of the pilot, how long the officer had been in captivity, when the recovery had occurred and the sequence of events leading up to the rescue. When the command refused to verify the leak, Fried filed a story anyway, using what he considered non-sensitive facts. Although the Defense Department prevailed upon his employer, the New York Daily News, to withhold publication, by that time the need for some sort of official statement had become obvious. The Director of Information, Seventh Air Force, Col. William McGinty, attempted to fill the vacuum by drafting a lengthy communique for MACV's approval and release. On instructions from the Defense Department, however, the command held its announcement to the barest minimum, stating only that a Navy pilot had been recovered after a period of Communist captivity and that his family was being notified. McGinty protested that the statement failed to give the Air Force proper credit for the rescue but the command refused to make any change.

Back in San Diego they treated him for kidney and liver disease. They fixed his teeth and then he got malaria - right there in the hospital - they cured him of that as well. At first he slept on the floor; a bed was just too soft. Then came the nightmares and he'd wake up three or four times a night sweating and screaming and yelling. What Dieter found was that this was the period of his life when he was most alive, *"Death didn't want me,"* he always explained.

In the autumn of 1966 he received the Sword of Loyola from the Loyola University, Chicago. The Sword of Loyola is Loyola University's highest honour. It is conferred upon an individual who holds to the spiritual qualities associated with St. Ignatius of Loyola: courage, dedication, and service. Previous recipients were Herbert Hoover (1964), Lt. Col. James A. McNulty and Maxime A. Faget (1965).

*Dieter Dengler at San Diego
Press conference September 1966*

*With his doctor Captain Alden Holmes at
San Diego Naval Hospital, he stayed in
the hospital for two months*

Lt (jg) Dengler shows the Secretary of State for the Navy Paul Nitze a Skyraider model where the flak hit the starboard wing, September 1966

Lieutenant Dieter Dengler USN

*San Diego California when Dieter meets his Mum, Maria
and his brother Klaus*

*Dieter Dengler prepares to enter
the cockpit of a Douglas
Skyhawk, Miramar*

(Eugene Deatrick)

Lieutenant Dieter Dengler meets his rescuer Colonel Eugene P. Deatrick.

A press conference was held at the Naval Air Station North Island, San Diego on 13 September 1966 at 10.08, with Dieter Dengler and his mother Mrs Maria Dengler and his brother Klaus present. He had another brother, Roland, who was a butcher in Calw. Dieter was introduced by Captain Duncan who explained the situation and how he was still receiving medical treatment on the sixth floor of Balboa Naval Hospital in San Diego. Dieter briefly spoke about what had happened, how he was rescued and of his gratitude for being alive - then he took questions from the press corps. Most of the questions concerned his survival, his physical surroundings, his diet and how he escaped. Most of the questions had to be rephrased by Captain Hill who also pointed out that most of the information was still classified. Dieter explained his background as a child in the Second World War, living in post war Germany and arriving in America in 1957. He was asked about his German passport and how Lieutenant Martin was killed. Dieter's training in escaping and survival at the navy survival school at Warner Springs, California, helped him survive as a prisoner and make escape plans despite intolerable torture. (The problem with the school was it was heavily westernised and did not take account of conditions in the Far East.) Dieter also explained how he was not brainwashed and the treatment he received was normal for the Laotian/Vietnamese guards. He explained how he had a handful of rice a day and anything that crawled or ran though the basha was food. He pointed out that he lost 59 pounds in captivity and that he weighed a cadaverous 98 pounds when he got back.

Dengler was then asked about the North Vietnamese air defences but Captain Hill intervened again saying it was a security matter. He was then asked about his fiancée Morena Adamich who lived in Belmont California and was a research assistant at Belmont Laboratories, Morena was present at the press conference. He explained how they wanted to be married and that a date had been set. He finished by saying that when he was escaping in the jungle all he wanted to do was get home and open a German style restaurant and never be hungry again. The conference finished at 11.20.

The wedding that was finally planned for 16 October was postponed due to his medical problems. Defying his doctors, he eloped to Reno with his fiancé, San Mateo classmate Marina Adamich. Later they opened a German restaurant on Mount Tamalpais, Marin County north of San Francisco.

By December 1966 he was making progress. He now weighed about 150 pounds the weakness had gone and his energy had returned. He had still some health issues: ringworm on his feet; there were internal parasites and he was temporarily losing his hair. He thought that in a few more weeks he would be able to fly again. If Dieter Dengler had not fled to freedom after a short captivity, he might well have perished in Laos's dark jungle shadows. Of some three hundred U.S. personnel listed as missing in action over Laos, only nine turned up on the capture rolls among those released during *Operation Homecoming,*

After recovering from his injuries, he served with the Commander Naval Air Forces Pacific from November 1966 to May 1967 and then with VC-7 at Miramar NAS San Diego, California, from May 1967 until he left active duty he entered the Naval Reserve on 1 February 1968. During this period he was promoted to full Lieutenant. He left the Naval Reserve on 16 February 1978 and he received the Navy Cross, Distinguished Flying Cross, Purple Heart, Prisoner of War Medal, Bronze Star and Air Medal. He then joined Trans-World Airlines, New York, initially as a flight engineer then he rose to airline pilot. Dieter was initially based in New York then San Francisco. He retired from TWA at the age of 59. He then became a private aircraft test pilot surviving four aircraft crashes - *"Death still did not want him."*

In 1997 a documentary was released concerning his captivity in Laos*, "Little Dieter needs to fly."* We first meet Dengler at a tattooist, he drives his antique car; he is haunted by his friend Duane Martin who speaks to him of his cold feet and then at his home in California, he is filled with excitement, obsessively opening and closing his door several times, looking at the camera wide eyed, staring, before explaining that the prison camp made him appreciate being able open a door and to come and go freely. Inside his house were several paintings of open doors. He showed the producer Werner Herzog his six-burner stove and well-stocked fridge and larder: then he prised

Dieter Dengler touring the aircraft carrier, USS Constellation, on December 1, 1996, in San Diego, California.

open the floorboards to reveal another hoard of rice, wheat, flour, honey, sugar and other food. Dieter would never starve again. Herzog took Dengler back to Laos, going so far as to march Dieter, handcuffed and under armed guard, through the jungle - all the old terror returned. In spite of his traumatic memories and ordeal, Dengler was a happy, informative guide, cheerfully demonstrating how to escape from handcuffs or to make a fire using only bamboo.

Dieter was married three times, first to Marina Adamich (1966 to March 1970), then Irene Lam (11 September, 1980 to 3 April, 1984), and finally Yukiko Dengler; he had two sons, Rolf and Alexander Dengler. He was an expert skier, judo enthusiast and surfboarder, even when the latter two were just getting started in California. His metal sculpture was always in demand in local art galleries. In 2000 he received a diagnosis of rapid onset of Amyotrophic Lateral

Sclerosis, also known as Lou Gehrig's disease, a disease that for some reason affects more military veterans than the general public, it's a degenerative illness. A motor neuron disease, loss of life typically continues until the abilities to eat, speak, move and lastly, breathe are all lost: Dieter Dengler, impeccably dressed, sitting in his electric wheel chair, on the driveway, there at the local fire station with a pistol, he committed suicide on 7 February 2001; on 19 March 2001, he was buried in Arlington National Cemetery with full military honours and a flypast of F-14 Tomcats with the, *"missing man"* formation to honour him. R.I.P.

USNAVY/ARLINGTONOFFICIAL/LOC/GM

Arlington 19 March 2001 F-14 Tomcat formation,
funeral of Dieter Dengler

Rescue Pilot
Eugene Peyton Deatrick Jr.
17 November 1924 – 30 December 2020 (age 96)

While serving in Vietnam as the commanding officer of the 1st Air Commando Squadron, he located and initiated the rescue of Navy Lt. Dieter Dengler who had escaped from a Laotian prison camp weeks before.

Eugene P. Deatrick Jr. was born 17 November 1924, in Pittsburgh, Pennsylvania, the only child of Dr. Lily Bell Sefton Deatrick and Dr. Eugene P. Deatrick, Sr. He grew up in Morgantown, West Virginia where his mother was a professor of Chemistry and his father a professor of Agriculture at West Virginia University. Deatrick graduated from Woodrow Wilson High School in Washington, D.C. in 1942. During his first year of college at West Virginia University, Deatrick enlisted in the Air Corps Reserve. He was nominated to the United States Military Academy by Senator Jennings Randolph in 1943. He graduated from the U.S. Military Academy at West Point in 1946. Deatrick entered the U.S. Army Air

Charles M. Simpson, Eugene P. Deatrick, and Lee Parmly
November 1966 Pleiku South Vietnam

Corps following graduation. Deatrick flew B-25s at Enid, Oklahoma then transitioned to the 307th Bomb Wing at MacDill AFB in Florida where he flew B-29s. From 1947 to 1948, he served a tour with the 10th Air Rescue Squadron in Adak, Alaska where he flew B-17s, L-5s, and PBY Catalinas. The noted Norwegian Arctic explorer, Colonel Bernt Balchen, was his commanding officer.

In 1949, he was assigned to the 3759th Electronics Test Squadron whose mission was the development of new radar bombing equipment. In 1950 the squadron moved to Eglin Air Force Base, Florida as the nucleus of the new Air Armament Centre. Deatrick was assigned as the Bomber Engineering Test Pilot. In addition to bombers, he flew the T-33, P-51 Mustang, and the F-84 Thunderjet. In 1951, Deatrick was a member of the first class to attend the newly formed Experimental Test Pilot School at Edwards Air Force Base, California, and subsequently served five years in the Bomber Flight Test Division at Wright Patterson AFB, Ohio. During this tour of duty, he flew development tests on the B-47 and B-52 aircraft among many other programmes

51

He then flew B-47 and B-52s during nuclear weapons effect tests at the Pacific Proving Grounds in 1954 (Operation Castle) and 1956 (Operation Redwing).

In 1966, he served in Pleiku where he assumed command of the 1st Air Commando Squadron. In Vietnam he flew more than 400 combat missions in the A-1 Skyraider. After returning home, he served as Commandant of the USAF Test Pilot School at Edwards Air Force Base from 1967-68. A graduate of the National War College, he earned a master's degree from George Washington University and served as Director of Test, Air Force Systems Command for two years before retiring from the Air Force in 1974.

In 1996, Deatrick portrayed himself in *Little Dieter Needs to Fly*, the Werner Herzog documentary about the escape and rescue of Dieter Dengler. In the documentary Dieter and Eugen dine together at Thanksgiving, reminiscing about the escape and rescue. In 1997, Deatrick was interviewed by the Air Force Historian, Richard P. Hallion, during the review of Operation TAILWIND. On March 9, 1999, on the thirty-third anniversary of the Battle of A Shau, Deatrick and other members of the 1st Air Commando Squadron gathered at a Pentagon ceremony to honour Bernie Fisher. In 2007, he attended the premier of *Rescue Dawn* at Andrews AFB and spoke of his role in Dengler's rescue. Prior to his death, he lived in Alexandria, Virginia. Deatrick's wife of 55 years, Zane, died in January 2012 and was buried in Arlington National Cemetery.

Eugene P. Deatrick at Edwards Air Force Base with a Lockheed F-104 Starfighter

During his career, Deatrick flew more than 50 different types of aircraft and accumulated more than 12000 hours of flying. His military decorations included the Legion of Merit with oak leaf cluster, the Distinguished Flying Cross with oak leaf cluster, the Bronze Star with valour device and oak leaf cluster and the Air Medal with 22 oak leaf clusters.

Eugene P. Deatrick was a member of the Society of Experimental Test Pilots (SETP), the International Order of Characters, the Order of Daedalians, the Air Force Association, the Quiet Birdmen, the Old Bold Pilots, and Silver Wings Over Washington. He served as President of the National Aviation Club for three years and received the National Aeronautic Association's Cliff Henderson Award for aviation achievement and the Wesley L. McDonald Elder Statesman of Aviation award. Deatrick was selected as the USAF Test Pilot School's Distinguished Alumnus in 2001 and was inducted into the Gathering of Eagles program. His career was documented by SETP and the West Point Centre for Oral History.

CVA-61 USS Ranger1966

3

USS *Ranger* (CVA-61)
Forrestal Class Aircraft Carrier

The aircraft carrying vessel has its roots in the early twentieth century when the idea was first discussed by Clement Ader and then developed in Scotland, at the Beardmore works, Dalmuir, by the Marquis of Graham. At Dalmuir the former liner *Conte Rosso* was converted to a flat top aircraft carrier HMS *Argus*. By 1939 the aircraft carrier was on the verge of supplanting the battleship in all major fleets. At the close of the Second World War the aircraft carrier was supreme, proving the concept of a floating carrier strike force.

USS *Ranger* (CVA-61) was a Forrestal-class super aircraft carrier. The vessel was an all-steel, all-welded combat ship built from 1954 to 1957 at Newport News, Virginia. At the time of her commissioning in 1957, *Ranger* was the largest, most powerful warship ever built. The planned cost for the vessel was 144 million dollars. The ship was 1067 feet long, 130 feet in the beam at the waterline and was divided into eleven decks with thousands of watertight compartments. *Ranger* was in service in the United States Navy for 37 years serving during the Cold War with the Soviet Union, extensively during the Vietnam War and at the end of her career against Iraq during Operation Desert Storm in 1991. Decommissioned in 1993, *Ranger* was in outstanding material condition internally, despite her weathered exterior cosmetic appearance, when laid up she retained nearly all of the original design construction.

Ranger was one of eight supercarriers built shortly after the Second World War. Built of 59650 tons of steel by more than 10000 shipbuilders of Newport News Shipbuilding in Newport News, Virginia, *Ranger*'s keel was laid down 2 August 1954, launched 29 September 1956, sponsored by Mrs. Arthur Radford, wife of Admiral Radford, Chairman of the Joint Chiefs of Staff; *Ranger* was commissioned at the Norfolk Naval Shipyard 10 August 1957, Capt. Charles T. Booth II, in command. USS *Ranger* was named after the

USS Ranger prepares for her Christening

Bow view of Ranger in the dock

Mrs. Arthur Radford, wife of Admiral Radford, Chairman of the Joint Chiefs of Staff, Christens USS Ranger 10 August 1957

CVA-61 Ship's plaque

*CVA-61 USS Ranger
outfitting Pier 29,
September 1956*

*Alongside Pier 29
September 1956*

CV-4 USS *Ranger* aircraft carrier of World War Two fame and the 1777 Sloop-of-war first commanded by John Paul Jones.

At the time, *Ranger* was the largest warship ever built; its size and power were unrivalled. *Ranger* was the first American carrier designed and constructed with an angled deck - a transformative British design innovation that is still in use today. By separating active and parked aircraft, the angled deck improved efficiency and safety of flight deck operations by enabling launch and landing to occur simultaneously and by preventing an aircraft from crashing into parked aircraft and causing a fire. Minor engineering adjustments included removing a notch at the stern; instead, the flight deck and after bulkhead continued directly to the transom. The sponsons were also differed in shape and size from the prior two supercarriers. *Ranger* was the only Forrestal-class carrier to retain its original gun sponsons, although the five-inch mounts were removed and replaced by surface-to-air missiles.

USS *Ranger* displaced 81000 tons - a 25% increase over the prior Midway class of aircraft carriers. The beam was 130 feet - nearly 20 feet greater. Hangar deck clearance was a full 25 feet versus the prior 17.5 feet. The carrier was built with four advanced steam catapults (a British innovation) instead of two obsolete hydraulic designs. The four steam-powered catapults, two C11 at the bow (numbers one and two from starboard to port) and two heavy C7 catapults at the waist (numbers three and four, starboard to port) on the port side. The port catapults were canted outward and toward one another, and permitted launches from the angled deck. Due to this positioning, they could not be used for simultaneous launch as could the bow catapults. The bow (forward) catapults measured 249ft long and could launch a 730000lb aircraft at 215mph. The waist catapults were 211ft long and were limited to 70000lb. *Ranger* and the other Forrestal class carrier *Independence* had four C11 catapults. At the end of catapults one and two were catapult overruns (resembling "horns"), called Van Velm bridle catchers, which facilitated the bridle system used to launch aircraft such as the F-8 Crusader, A-4 Skyhawk and F-4 Phantom II. The overruns would catch the bridle after launch allowing for re-use.

The electronics suite included mast, radar and communications antennas which were located on the island superstructure. This configuration provided much better radar coverage than the layout in the original design, which called for a series of radars to be located around the carrier and merged into one radar picture. Forrestal's radar systems on commissioning were simple. Air search was provided by the SPS-8A and SPS-12 (2-D) radar. Saratoga and *Ranger* shared this configuration, although Independence, the last of the Forrestal class, received the newer SPS-8B and SPS-37A (2-D). These radars were replaced in the early 1960s by the SPS-43A (2-D) and SPS-30 (3-D), which assumed the duties of the SPS-8A/B and SPS-12. All of the class used the SPN-10 navigation radar.

Ranger's then state-of-the art 1200 psi high pressure steam plant with eight boilers was powerful - the four engines, developed 280000 horsepower, with four 21-foot propellers which could drive the ship at 35 knots. Two 45-ton rudders enabled the *Ranger* to make sharp, fast turns, for which the ship was renowned. *Ranger* was designed with four aircraft lifts. The port side lift, weighing 105 tons, was the largest and heaviest all-welded aluminium structure built to date.

USS Ranger joined the Atlantic Fleet on 3 October 1957. She conducted air operations, individual ship exercises and final acceptance trials along the eastern seaboard of the United States and in the Caribbean Sea until June 20, 1958. The ship then departed Norfolk Naval Base for its new homeport of Alameda, California, arriving on 20 August. The carrier spent the remaining part of the year in pilot qualification training for Air Group 14 and fleet exercises off the California coast.

On a westward passage of the ship around Cape Horn in July 1958 at the request of the Bureau of Ships, *Ranger* was fitted with transducers to measure strains, pressures and ship motions. Strain gauges were also installed and accelerometers fitted near the bow at the centre of gravity and at the touchdown point on the flight deck. She arrived on 20 August 1958 at the Naval Air Station in Alameda, California via South America; this was to be her home port for the following five years.

USS Ranger South China Sea 15 June 1966

On 10 November 1958 Ranger suffered an explosion in the magazine area seven decks below the waterline while off San Francisco, California, killing two. A careless act by two crewmen trying to obtain gunpowder from the magazine to fuel a miniature ram jet engine they had built caused the explosion. The Navy said the two men were known rocket enthusiasts and were not authorized to be in the magazine area at the time of the explosion. The *"relatively minor"* damage took about a month to repair due to the location of the accident.

During her first western Pacific deployment in 1959, *Ranger* launched more than 7000 sorties in support of Seventh Fleet operations. With Carrier Air Group 9 embarked, the ship departed Alameda 6 February 1960, for a second western Pacific deployment and returned home on 30 August. From 11 August 1961 to 8 March 1962, *Ranger* deployed to the Far East for a third time. USS *Ranger* departed Alameda 9 November 1962, for a brief operation off the coast of Hawaii, and then proceeded, via Okinawa, to the Philippines. Returning to homeport from the Far East 14 June she underwent

Douglas A-4 Skyhawk

overhaul in the San Francisco Naval Shipyard 7 August to the 10 February 1964.

(On 5 April 1963 *Ranger* suffered an explosion and fire in the boiler uptakes while en route from Beppu, Japan, to Iwakuni, Japan.)

Although *Ranger* had many roles over its life, her combat record was both enduring and impressive. Deployed in combat from its earliest days until the very end of its active life, the ship amassed a battle record equalled by few ships. In May 1964, while observing the French nuclear detonation at Mururoa in the Pacific, *Ranger* launched a U-2 spy plane from its deck. It was reported that the launch, controlled by the intelligence agency, was deemed so secret that the flight deck personnel were sent below deck for the launch.

In August 1964 during her fifth cruise she was called for her first combat duty. Then on 15 April 1965 she had an engine room fire killing one. In early 1966 she served at Dixie Station off the Vietnamese coast. A move to Yankee Station from 21 January - 10 February brought an unfortunate loss of aircraft due to both accidents and combat operations against North Vietnam. One Douglas A4E Skyhawk of *VA-55* was lost at sea following catapult launch (the pilot was recovered uninjured), while a Douglas A4C Skyhawk of

Skyraider 04 Down

Douglas Skyraider

McDonnell F-4 Phantom II

Royal Navy Sea Vixen from HMS Hermes lands on the USS Ranger 16 January 1963

1966 Refit

USS Ranger seaward the great ship

Refit at Hunter's Point

Refit 1974

Douglas Skywarrior flight refuelling a North American RA-5C

*Kuddles, the 1966 ship's mascot who would
inspect the ship accompanied by cakes*

VA-146, and two Skyraiders of VA-145 were lost in combat action with the three pilots (including Dieter Dengler) and one NFO missing or unaccounted for. After a 38 day bombing pause against targets in North Vietnam, President Lyndon B. Johnson again resumed the bombing on 31 January 1966. The pilots of VA-145 and Air Wing 14 were extremely busy as several lucrative targets, such as trucks, lines of communication, and North Vietnamese troop areas, were assigned for sortie attacks.

Later the carrier made seven deployments to the waters off Vietnam. In 1967, the carrier was the first to deploy the new A-7 Corsair II - a light bomber designed to replace the A-4 Skyhawk.

Although *Ranger*'s list of combat activities is long (20 deployments of 90 days or more), the ship's two major combat operations occurred during the Vietnam War era and the Gulf War. *Ranger* was deployed to the Western Pacific from commissioning to 1974:

20 Jun 1958 - 20 Aug 1958

3 Jan 1959 - 27 Jul 1959

Ranger launched more than 7000 sorties in support of Seventh Fleet operations:

6 Feb 1960 - 30 Aug 1960

11 Aug 1961- 9 Mar 1962

9 Nov 1962 - 14 Jun 1963

In January 1963, *Ranger* conducted joint flight exercises with HMS Hermes (R 12); U.S. Navy F-4 Phantoms landed aboard Hermes and Royal Navy Sea Vixens landed aboard *Ranger*.

May 1964

During this brief deployment to the South Pacific, *Ranger* became the only aircraft carrier to conduct operational U-2 flights.

5 Aug 1964 - 6 May 1965

Ranger became flagship of Rear Admiral Miller who commanded Fast Carrier Task Force 77 and helped the Seventh Fleet maintain open sea-lanes.

On 15 Mar 1965, aircraft from *Ranger* joined 34 U.S. Air Force fighter-bombers to attack an ammunition depot in Hanoi.

At 271 days, this deployment was *Ranger*'s longest.

10 Dec 1965 - 25 Aug 1966

Attack Carrier Air Wing 14 flew the first strikes against petroleum, oil, and lubricant storage facilities near Haiphong.26

In February 1966 *Ranger* aviator, Lt (jg.) Dieter Dengler was shot down over Laos. He initiated, planned and led an organized escape from a POW camp, becoming the longest-held U.S. pilot to escape captivity during the Vietnam War. Two films were made about Lt. Dengler, a documentary, *Little Dieter wants to fly* and *Rescue Dawn*, starring Christian Bale. The book, Hero Found also describes these events.

During this deployment, *Ranger* was awarded both a Navy Unit Commendation and the Arleigh Burke Fleet Trophy for battle efficiency. "Our Navy" magazine also named *Ranger* the 1966 Ship of the Year. 4 Nov 1967 - 25 May 1968.

In preparation for this deployment, *Ranger* logged its 88000th carrier landings and became the first carrier to deploy with the Vought A-7A Corsair II attack aircraft.

Ranger's cooperation with USAF continued during this deployment; Air Force personnel were aboard during the entire cruise to evaluate the A-7A aircraft.

In January 1968, *Ranger* was diverted for one month to the Yellow Sea in attempt to rescue the USS Pueblo, which had been captured by the North Koreans.

26 Oct 1968 - 17 May 1969

Ranger received its second Navy Unit Commendation for this deployment.

14 Oct 1969 - 1 June 1970

USS *Ranger* never underwent a comprehensive Service Life Extension, the ship did undergo many post-deployment refurbishments during its long life of service and all of those also occurred on the West Coast - in San Francisco (1963-1964, 1965), Bremerton (1966-1967, 1968, 1977-1978, and 1984-1985). From 10 July 1993, *Ranger* was berthed at Naval Inactive Ship Maintenance Facility, Bremerton, Washington. Plans in 2004 to convert her to a museum at Portland Oregon came to nothing. It was hoped to place a dedication plaque to Dieter Dengler on the ship. On 22 December 2014, the Navy awarded the contract for the towing and demolition of

Servicing a Phantom

Preparation for painting   *Skyraider inspection*

CVA-61 USS *Ranger*, to International Shipbreaking Ltd., for $0.01, the lowest price possible for that type of work. Ranger left Bremerton, Washington, on 5 March 2015 for International Shipbreaking Ltd.'s facility in Brownsville, Texas. She then set out once more, this time in the opposite direction from her maiden voyage decades before and made the 16000 mile passage and arrived in Brownsville after a six month long journey, as she had to be towed around South America since she was much too large for passage through the Panama Canal.

Some of Ranger's many awards include one Humanitarian Service Medal, three Navy Unit Commendations, five Meritorious Unit Commendations, three Battle "E" Awards, 15 Armed Forces Expeditionary Medals, and 25 Vietnam Service Medals. More than 100,000 sailors and marines served aboard Ranger during her long and illustrious career.

CVA-61 USS Ranger leaves Bremerton March 2015 for demolition

Designed Specification

Standard displacement: 61100 tons
Light displacement: 56000 tons
Length: 1046 feet
Maximum width: 252 feet
Beam (hull): 130 feet
Maximum navigation draught: about 37 feet
Number of boilers: 8
Shaft horsepower: 280000
Rated speed: over 30 knots
Crew: 4104 plus
Aircraft: 70 plus
Contract price: $128832893.17
Contract cost: $117570808.90
Profit: $11262084.27
Source: Board of Contract Appeals Decisions by United States.
Armed Services Board of Contract Appeals.1971 Commerce Clearing
House. Inc.

USS Ranger

In Command 1963 to 1969

Captain George C. Duncan   7 May 1962 to 20 May 1963

Captain William E. Lemos   20 May 1963 to 28 May 1964

Captain Alton B. Grimes   28 May 1964 to 10 May 1965

Captain Leo B. McCuddin   10 May 1965 to 7 June 1966

Captain William M. Harnish   7 June 1966 to 20 October 1966

Captain William M. Donnelly Jr. 20 October 1966 to 27 March 1968

Captain William H. Livingston   27 March 1968 to 28 June 1969

USS RANGER (CVA-61) Vietnam Operations
(Covering 1964 to 1966)

Deployment Dates to Vietnam: 5 August 1964 - 6 May1965
Source: *Ranger* history report for 1 Apr - 30 Sep 1964, 1 Oct 1964 -
31 Mar 1965 and 31 Mar 1965 – 30 Sep 1965.

These reports provide very limited information regarding port visits.
In-port, Subic Bay circa Aug - Sep 1964 for three weeks of boiler
repair.
In-port, Yokosuka, Japan circa late Sep - 13 Nov 1964
In-port, Hong Kong circa 30 Dec 1964 - 6 Jan 1965
In-port, Subic Bay circa 7-8 Jan 1965
7 February 1965: In Operation Flaming Dart I, 49 planes from *Coral
Sea* (CVA-43)*, Hancock* (CVA-19) and *Ranger* (CVA 61) bomb
North Vietnamese barracks and staging areas near Dong Hoi.
10 - 11 February 1965: In Operation Flaming Dart II, over 100 planes
from *Ranger, Coral Sea,* and *Hancock* strike North Vietnamese
barracks and staging areas at Cahn Hoa.
15 March: Seventh Fleet initiates Operation Market Time. The U.S.
Navy also launches the first non-retaliatory strike of war, in which
pilots from *Ranger* and *Hancock* hit an ammunition depot at Phu Qui.
In-port, Subic Bay 19 Mar - circa 30 Mar 1965.
Inport, Subic circa 15-20 Apr 1965
Deployment Dates: 10 December1965 - 25 August 1966

Source: Ranger Cruise Report for above dates.
Inport, Pearl Harbour 16 Dec 1965
Inport, Pearl Harbour 19 Dec 1965
Inport, Pearl Harbour 24 - 27 Dec 1965
Inport, Subic Bay 10 - 11Jan1966
Inport, Subic Bay 13 - 21 Feb 1966
Inport, Yokosuka 26 Mar - 4 Apr 1966
Inport, Yokosuka 12 - 20 May 1966
Inport, Yokosuka 22 - 24 May 1966
Inport, Subic Bay 1 - 10Jul 1966
Inport, Subic Bay 8 Aug 1966
Carrier Deployments During the Vietnam Conflict
Inport, Yokosuka 12 - 15Aug 1966

USS Ranger (CVA-61)
Aircraft losses Vietnam
1964 to 1966

9 December 1964: RA-5C 149306 RVAH-5
15 March 1965: A-IH 135375 VA-95
9 April 1965: F-4B 151425 VF-96
        F-4B 151403 VF-96
11 April 1965: A-IH 135226 VA-95
16 January 1966: RA-5C 149312 RVAH-9
25 January 1966: A-4E 152021 VA-55
31 January 1966: A-4E 152066 VA-55
1 February 1966: A-IJ 142031 VA-145
        Lt(jg.) Dieter Dengler (POW - escaped)
        A-4C 149527 VA-146
10 February 1966: A-IH 137627 VA-145
1 March1966: F-4B 150443 VF-143
        A-4E I52057 VA-55
23 April 1966: A-4E 152025 VA-55
30 April 1966: A-4E 151145 VA-55
2 May1966: A-4E 151034 VA-55
5 May1966: A-4C 149571 VA-146

1 June 1966: A-4E 151057 VA-55
15 June 1966: F-4B 152251 VF-143
     . A-4E 152063 VA-55
20 June 1966: A-IH 139806 VA-145
25 June 1966: A-4C 149567 VA-146
11 July 1966: F-4B 152262 VF-143
15 July 1966: A-4E IS1024 VA-SS
24 July 1966: A-4E 150040 VA-55
3 August 1966: A-1H 134586 VA-145
[Source: Vietnam Air Losses, Hobson, C, Midland Publishing, 2001,
ISBN 1 85780 115 6]

Naval Squadrons

(1)

Ranger (CVA 61) with CVW-9 (5 Aug 1964 - 6 May 1965)

VF-92 F-4B	VAW-11 Det M E-1B
VF-96 F-4B	VAH-2 Det M A-3B
VA-93 A-4C	HU-1 D1 Unit M UH-2A
VA-95 A-1J & A-1H	*VAP-61 Det RA-3B
VA-94 A-4C	*VQ-1 Det EA-3B
RVAH-5 RA-5C	
VFP-63 Det M RF-8A	

(2)

Ranger (CVA 61) with CVW-14 (10 Dec 1965 - 25 Aug 1966)

VF-142 F-4B	VAH-2 Det F A-3B
VF-143 F-4B	VAW-11 Det F E-2A
VA-145 A-1H & A-1J	HC-1 D1 Unit F UH-2A & UH-2B
VA-146 A-4C	
VA-55 A-4E	*VQ-1 Det EA-3B
RVAH-9 RA-5C	*VAP-61 Det RA-3B

* These squadron detachments were not aboard the carrier for the entire
  Deployment

Skyraiders with Phantoms deck view 1966

The first XBTD-1 (09085) spring 1945

4

Douglas AD-1 Skyraider

The Douglas Skyraider was the brainchild of Ed. Heinemann a draughtsman at the Douglas Aircraft Company. Heinemann had joined the company in 1926 and was responsible for the design of nineteen aircraft and many other aircraft components. The Douglas Company was formed in 1920 and before the Second World War had also designed the Douglas Sleeper Transport which evolved into the legendary DC-3 or C-47 Dakota in Military service. The headquarters of the company was at Santa Monica California with other divisions at Long Beach, Cal.; Tulsa, Oklahoma; and Charlotte, North Carolina: the aircraft division was at Long Beach California. Douglas occupied the factory site at Clover Field, Santa Monica, California from 1928. The plant was repeatedly enlarged and comprised eight acres of land with 350000 square feet of floor space in buildings and adjoined an all paved surface flying field. At the time Douglas had a subsidiary interest in the Northrop Corporation, employing 1000 people at a factory of 140,209 square feet floor space at Los Angeles Municipal Airport.

Prototype Skyraider

In early 1944, the El Segundo design team led by Heinemann designed a replacement for the SBD Dauntless dive bomber. The United States Navy had a requirement for a carrier-based, single-engine, long-range, high-performance dive bomber. By June 1944, Douglas Company came up with plans for a new design. The Navy approved the concept and awarded Douglas a contract for 15 evaluation aircraft, which were given the designation XBT2D1 and named *"Dauntless II."*

Less than a year later the Dauntless II made its first flight on 18 March 1945, and shortly thereafter went to the Naval Air Test Centre. Navy test pilots took an immediate liking to the airplane, citing its superior balance and responsiveness to control input at all speeds, which meant excellent carrier wave-off capability.

Shortly after Heinemann began designing the XBT2D-1 a study was issued showing that for every 100 lb of weight reduction, the take-off run was decreased by 8 ft. the combat radius increased by 22 miles and the rate-of-climb increased by 18 ft./min. Heinemann immediately had his design engineers begin a program for finding weight savings on the XBT2D-1 design, no matter how small. Simplifying the fuel system resulted in a reduction of 270 lb; 200 lb by eliminating the internal bomb bay and hanging external stores from the wings or fuselage; 70 lb by using a fuselage dive brake; and 100 lb by using an older tailwheel design. In the end, Heinemann and his design engineers achieved more than 1,800 lb of weight reduction on the original XBT2D-1 design.

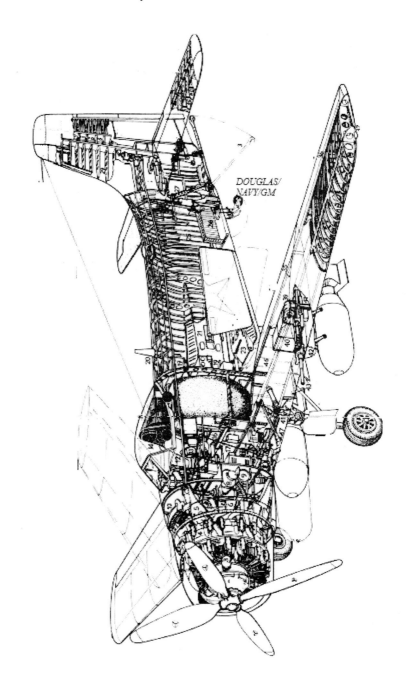

DOUGLAS/
NAVY/GM

The aircraft was a large, sturdy single-engine aeroplane with a length of 39 feet and a 50 foot wing span. Its empty weight was 10740 pounds. Its wings folded hydraulically overhead, reducing the wing span to 24 feet. Unique to the airframe were dive brakes built into the sides and bottom of its fuselage, thereby simplifying the wing structure. The huge dive brakes kept 500 mph dives in the safer region of 300 mph. Douglas doing away with the bomb bay reduced weight by 200 pounds. External stores would induce drag and the designers felt that the speed of an aeroplane with no bomb bay and empty racks was more important when exiting the target area. External attachment points also allowed for more flexibility in the types of stores that could be carried.

The Douglas designers, in a weight saving exercise, used the simpler, lighter tail wheel configuration. Its main landing gear retracted rearward and rotated 90 degrees for flush storage in the wings. Armour plating protected the cockpit area and a 20mm cannon was installed in each wing. The Dauntless II had three bomb racks: one on the fuselage centreline and one on each wing. The aircraft had distinctive large straight wings with seven hard points apiece. The Skyraider had excellent manoeuvrability at low speed and carried a large amount of ordnance over a considerable combat radius. It had a long loiter time for its size, compared to much heavier subsonic or supersonic jets. The aircraft was optimized for ground attack and was armoured against ground fire in key locations,

Power was supplied by a Wright R-3350-24 radial engine delivering 2500 horsepower at 2900 rpm for take-off. This engine was used to power the Boeing B-29 Superfortress atomic bomber. A huge 13 foot, 6 inch diameter Aeroproducts variable-pitch, constant-speed hollow steel propeller permitted a rapid rate of climb at steep angles. The aircraft was clean, simple, and functional reflecting the talent of Douglas engineers. In keeping with Heinemann's weight saving doctrine, it was 5000 pounds lighter than its nearest competitor. The lighter weight design requirement was met by first reducing the guaranteed design gross weight from 18000 to 16500 lb. To ensure that this figure would not be exceeded the designers were instructed to shoot for an additional weight reduction of 750 lb. The

Early Skyraider124129 in U.S. Navy service

Formation of Skyraiders about 1950

405 crashes

Fitting rockets 1952 during the Korean War

Skyraider with rocket and bomb armament

Preparing take off

success of their efforts was proven by the first flight of the BT2D-1 which was made with a weight of over 1000 lb. less than the guaranteed figure. Unfortunately, much of its structure later proved weak and a great deal of strengthening was necessary which added much of the weight saved in the initial design.

One month after its maiden flight, the U.S. Navy placed an order for 548 aircraft, which was reduced to 277 when the war with Japan ended. After service trials at NAS Alameda, California, 20, XBT2D-ls underwent landing gear strengthening and were assigned to VA-19A in the Pacific. In February 1946 the Dauntless II was renamed the Skyraider. When the Navy revised its aircraft designation system in April 1946, the BT2D became simply "AD" (Attack, Douglas) which, in the phonetic alphabet of that period, translated appropriately to "Able Dog." Production ADs were delivered to VA-3B and VA-4B, which put the Skyraider through carrier qualification aboard the USS *Sicily* during mid-1947. (Later in 1948 USS *Sicily* came to King George V Dock, Glasgow, to deliver Lockheed Shooting Stars to Europe.) By October 1947, AD-1s were aboard the USS *Midway* for cruises in the Atlantic and Mediterranean.

Success with the AD-1 through AD-3 series led to the AD-4, of which 1051 were built, more than any other in the design series; it also spawned the many sub-variants. Among the improvements introduced in the AD-4 was an autopilot, multi-seating, and additional armament. Later came the AD-4W early warning Skyraider, the AD-5 multi seat attack bomber and the AD-6. A total of 668 AD-5s were built, with the last one rolling off the production line in April 1956.

Under the Mutual Defense Aid Program (MDAP), the first exported Skyraiders went to Great Britain's Royal Navy beginning in 1951 to fulfil the Royal Navy's need for early warning carrier aircraft. A total of 50 AD-4Ws were acquired, which the Royal Navy designated AEW-ls. Initially twelve AEW-ls were purchased by Sweden after being converted to target tugs at Scottish Aviation and operated by Swedair under contract to the Swedish Air Force. During February 1960 the first of 113 Skyraider variants were delivered to the French Armee de l'Air, which flew them in support of French

1957-58 carrying a special store

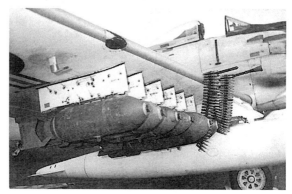

Bomb armament

Skyraider crash at Da Nang

Vietnamese Air Force Douglas Skyraider

South Vietnamese Air Force Da Nang 1967

forces in Algeria. In 1976 France sent six AD-4s to Chad, where they were flown by French mercenaries until 1984.

The later AD-6 reverted to the single-seat design for the day attack mission. The "Six" combined features of the AD-4B and AD-5, plus refinements that broadened its mission. Like the AD-4B, it was nuclear capable. The AD-6 was equipped for low-level bombing and it had the stores provisions developed for the AD-5; they were a centreline pylon and a stub pylon on each wing, just inboard of the wing fold-joint (for fuel tanks and heavy ordnance), and six racks on each outer wing. The Six also had a strengthened centre section and armour plate on the sides and bottom of the cockpit. Other improvements included simplified electronics and all-weather instruments. The AD-6 was powered by the Wright R-3350-26WA, which produced 2700 hp for a top speed of 343 mph. Its service ceiling was 28,500 feet and it had a combat range of 1,143 nautical miles. A total of 713 were produced. The last model was the AD-7 with a strengthened wing and a more powerful R-3350-26WB engine was installed. The AD-7's service ceiling was 25400 feet and it had a combat range of 1128 nautical miles.

The Douglas Skyraider's initial active service was during the Korean conflict from 1950. Designed to carry a bomb load of 1000lbs in some Korean operational sorties it flew with a load of 10500lbs. The last of 3180 Skyraiders rolled off the Douglas assembly line on 18 February 1957. A total of 28 sub-variants grew from the seven basic models. Under the 1962 Department of Defense re-designation system the AD-5, AD-5N, AD-5W, and AD-5Q became the A-1E, A1G, EA-IE, and EA-IF, respectively, while the AD-6 became the A-IH and the AD-7 became the A-lJ. The AD-5, -6, and -7 variants went to war in Southeast Asia.

Two A-1Es on loan from the US Navy were evaluated by U.S.A.F. Tactical Air Command's Special Air Warfare Centre (SAWC) at Eglin AFB, Florida, from August 1962 to January 1963. Then the U.S.A.F., at their Special Air Warfare Centre, Nellis Air Force Base, Nevada evaluated many aircraft or modified aircraft to find replacements for the T-28s and B-26s. The A-IE (AD-5) was found to be exceptionally well suited for the requirements of this particular

South Vietnam showing Skyraider air bases

situation and arrangements were made to obtain the U.S. Navy's inventory of the multi seat Skyraider. The aircraft were quickly run through a modification centre where dual controls (the U.S.N. A-IE had only single control), substitution of radio and navigational gear compatible with U.S.A.F. operation and other minor modifications were made. In June 1964 these aircraft were available for aggressive action in South Vietnam.

The first aircraft delivered to the USAF were A-1Es in mid-1964. After numerous programme changes 25 Skyraiders went to Tactical Air Command (TAC) to be used for Skyraider upgrade training at Hurlburt Field, Florida. A further 48 USAF A-1Es were at Bien Hoa AB by the end of 1964, by that time eight Skyraiders had been lost with the death of six American pilots and two Vietnamese observers. In August 1965 it was decided to camouflage the aircraft.

The Republic of Vietnam Air Force was provided with aircraft from the U.S. Navy stockpile at Litchfield, Arizona; twenty five AD-6 Skyraiders were provided in 1960 to replace its squadron of ageing F8F Bearcats through the Military Assistance Program (MAP). In addition to the Bearcats the Vietnamese Air Force had two squadrons of C-47 s and two squadrons of L-19s.The first of the Skyraiders arrived in Saigon on 24 September 1960 and after modification, processing and flight testing, they were flown from Tan Son Nhut AB to Bien Hoa AB to enter service with the VNAF. Over the next six years, further deliveries added a sufficient number of A-1s to allow the equipment of four additional squadrons. By January 1966 the VNAF had 146 Skyraiders in service.

In retaliation for attacks by the North Vietnamese in the Gulf of Tonkin on U.S. destroyers on 2 and 4 August 1964, President Johnson ordered strikes against North Vietnamese naval bases and petroleum storage depots. On 5 August the first U.S. strikes against North Vietnam were launched from the carriers USS *Constellation* and *Ticonderoga*. Besides F-8 Crusaders and A-4 Skyhawks, Skyraiders of Attack Squadron 52 (VA-52) aboard the "*Tico*," and VA-145 aboard the "*Connie*," did their part in amassing 64 sorties, which severely damaged or destroyed 25 patrol boats and 9 petroleum storage tanks.

A-1 H Skyraider "Bubbles n' Bust" March 1970

Skyraider being delivered to Vietnam by lighter

Two Spads with an MH-53 Super Jolly Green Giant

The A-1 carried four fixed forward firing 20mm cannons internally mounted in the wings and often carried additional 7.62 mm gun pods. Common bomb loads in included Mk-82 Snake eye and napalm canisters: the A-1 was capable of up to 8000 pounds of external ordnance. Most tactics included medium altitude dive bombing attacks with recovery above 200 feet above ground level. The Skyraider was capable of day and night operations. One final store was the Madden Kit. This was not a weapon but rather a 'survival kit' that contained items - maps, a survival radio and/or batteries, signalling devices, water or food - that a downed airman needed to facilitate his rescue. The store chosen was a kit with high drag fins that would slow the canister down before impact. It was painted bright yellow so that it would be easily spotted among the green vegetation of the jungle.

The A-1 Skyraider was well-suited for several combat operations in South Vietnam, flying rescue, close air support and forward air control (FAC) missions. In the rescue role the Skyraider pilot was required to locate the downed airman and protect him with the A-1's firepower. The pilot became the on scene commander of the recovery effort, controlling fighter-bomber strikes on hostile positions and escorting the helicopters during the pickup of the survivor. On a close air support mission the Skyraider pilot's ability to attack ground targets with pinpoint accuracy made the A-1 an outstanding weapon to support friendly troops in contact with the enemy. In the FAC role, the A-1 pilot was an aerial observer and controller. In constant radio contact with Army units in his sector, he warned of enemy ambushes and then controlled fast-moving fighters in strikes on the hostile positions. The airman downed deep in enemy territory and the embattled foot soldier caught in a Vietcong (VC) crossfire often depended on the Skyraiders for their very lives.

The Skyraider was capable of both night and daytime operations. In addition to the United States Navy the Skyraider few with the United States Air Force and the air force of South Vietnam, the last A-1 Skyraider leaving active service in 1971. Losses for the Skyraider in Vietnam were 256, 198 in combat and 58 non-combats. 144 Pilots were lost from both services, Air Force and Navy during the conflict.

Dieter Dengler's Squadron
VA-145
Lineage

Established as Reserve Attack Squadron SEVEN
HUNDRED TWO (VA-702) on 1 December 1949.
Reserve Attack Squadron SEVEN HUNDRED TWO
(VA-702) called to active duty on 20 July 1950 (Korea).
Redesignated Attack Squadron ONE HUNDRED
FORTY FIVE (VA-145) on 4 February 1953. Dis-established on 1
October 1993. The first squadron to be assigned the VA-145
designation.

Nickname: Rustlers, 1951-1954. Swordsmen, 1954-1993.

VA-145
Squadron Service
on board
Carrier Vessels

USS *Boxer* (CV-9): March 1951 close air support Korea, Operational
in the Formosa Strait April 1951, Interdiction Korea
USS *Kearsarge* (CVA-33) 16 Oct 1952: Commander B. T. Simonds,
the squadron's commanding officer, was lost when his plane crashed
into the water immediately following its launch.
USS *Ranger* (CVA-61) Jun - Aug 1958: The squadron was embarked
for its transit from Norfolk, via Cape Horn to its new home port at
Alameda.
USS *Ranger* (CVA-61) 5-8 Jul 1959: The squadron flew sorties from
the carrier while it operated off Taiwan due to increasing tensions
between the Chinese Nationalists and Chinese Communists.
USS *Ranger* (CVA-61) Jun 1964 - Jan 1965: The squadron
participated in Yankee Team Operations, flying Rescue Combat Air
Patrols in South Vietnam and Laos.
USS *Ranger* (CVA-61) 5 Aug 1964: VA-145 participated in
Operation Pierce Arrow, air strikes against North Vietnam in

retaliation for the attacks on the American destroyers USS *Turner Joy* (DD 951) and USS *Maddox* (DD 731) in the Gulf of Tonkin on 4 August. The squadron's Skyraiders, along with other aircraft from the air wing, struck torpedo boats and other targets at Hon Gay, North Vietnam. A second sortie of squadron aircraft, along with Skyhawks from VA-144, attacked five enemy naval vessels that were at sea, near the Lach Chao Estuary and Hon Me Island. The two vessels attacked by VA-145 were left dead in the water and smoking. During this attack Lieutenant (jg.) Richard C. Sather was shot down. He was the first naval aviator lost in the Vietnam Conflict.

USS *Ranger* (CVA-61) 31 Jan 1966: The squadron's commanding officer, Commander H. F. Griffith, was awarded the Silver Star for his actions as a flight leader directing and coordinating simultaneous attacks, under extremely adverse weather conditions against a heavily defended primary enemy line of communications and for his participation in the successful rescue of a downed naval aviator.

1 Feb 1966: During one of the squadron's combat missions over North Vietnam, Lieutenant (jg.) Dieter Dengler was shot down. He was captured in Laos and imprisoned. On 30 June 1966 he escaped from a prisoner-of-war stockade, was rescued and returned to the squadron on 21 July. For his daring escape he was awarded the Navy Cross.

USS *Ranger* (CVA-61) Jun - Nov 1967: During 120 days on Yankee Station, the squadron assisted in the recovery of 14 downed airmen, both Navy and Air Force.

USS *Enterprise* (CVAN-65) 16 Apr 1969: with VA-145 embarked, departed Yankee Station en-route to Korean waters in response to the downing of a VQ-1 EC-121 aircraft by the North Koreans on 15 April. The squadron operated in the Sea of Japan and the Yellow Sea until 11 May.

10 Dec 1965 - 25 Aug 1966: CVW-14 CVA-61 (*Ranger*) A-1H/J WestPac/Vietnam

11 May 1967 - 30 Dec 1967: CVW-10 CVS-11 (*Intrepid*) A-1H Med/IO/West Pac/Vietnam

06 Jan 1969 - 02 Jul 1969: CVW-9 CVAN-65* (*Enterprise*) A-6A/B WestPac/Vietnam

27 Oct 1970 - 17 Jun 1971: CVW-2 CVA-61 (*Ranger*) A-6A/C WestPac/Vietnam
16 Nov 1972 - 23 Jun 1973: CVW-2 CVA-61 (*Ranger*) A-6A/B & KA-6D WestPac/Vietnam
07 May 1974 - 18 Oct 1974: CVW-2 CVA-61 (*Ranger*) A-6A & KA-6D WestPac
* The squadron was temporarily shore based at NAS Barbers Point from January to March 1969 following a fire on *Enterprise* (CVAN-65) on 14 January 1969. The carrier was repaired at Pearl Harbour and was en-route to WestPac on 11 March with VA-145 embarked.

A-1H
In squadron service with
VA-145-1966

A-IH 134586 VA-145/515; was hit by small arms fire over Quang Ninh Province, North Vietnam, on 3 August 1966. The pilot, Lt. D. Franz, was able to fly out over the Gulf of Tonkin where he bailed out and was rescued.
A-IH 134589 VA-145/504; VA-25/403
A-IH 135338 VA-145/505; VA-I 65/205 "Glider Rider"
A-IH 135370 VA-145/506
A-IH 137559 VA-52/309; VA-145/502
A-IH 137570 VA-145
A-IH 137616 VA-145/511
A-IH 137622 VA-145/510 and 512: VA-521386; VA-251406
A-IH 137627 VA-145/506; crashed near target during armed recon mission North Vietnam on 10 February 1966, Ll. Gary D. Hopps KIA.
A-IH 139680 VA-25/581: VA-145; VA-165/210
A-IH 139691 VA-145/505; VA-25
A-IH 139702 VA-145/513; VA-196/601
A-IH 139760 VA-145;crashed into sea during low-angle rocket attack on torpedo boat North Vietnam on 5 August 1964, Lt. jg. Richard C. Sather KIA, (first USN A-I loss in South East Asia.)

A-1H 139806 VA-145; crashed into sea following launch from carrier on 20 June 1966, Lt. Cmdr. John W. Tunnell killed

A-lH 139820 VA-145/506

A-1J 142016 VA-145/507; VA-l15/50l (experimental camouflage 1966)

A-1J 142028 VA-I 76/402; VA-145/504

A-1J 142031 VA-145/504; crash-landed in Laos after damaged by AAA on 1 February 66, Lt jg. Dieter Dengler captured, but escaped on 29 June 1966 and was rescued 20 July 1966

A-1J 142033 VA-145/501 "Baby"

A-IJ 142065 VA-145; VA-165/200

Aircraft Assigned

Aircraft	Date
TBM	1949
AD-2	Aug 1950
AD-4Q	Sep 1950
AD-1	Dec 1951
AD-4L	Apr 1952
AD-3Q	Apr 1953
AD-4B	Apr 1953
AD-4NA	Aug 1954
AD-5	Oct 1954
AD-6/A-1H*	Feb 1956
A-6A	04 Jun 1968
A-6B	06 Aug 1968
A-6C	11 May 1970
KA-6D	1972
A-6E	22 Sep 1976
A-6E TRAM†	30 Nov 1981

* The AD-6 designation was changed to A-1H in 1962.

† The A-6E TRAM version was capable of carrying and firing the Harpoon missile (an anti-ship missile)

Royal Navy AEW-1 Skyraider

THE SCOTTISH AVIATION/DOUGLAS
SKYRAIDER TARGET TOWING CONVERSION

In February 1962, the Swedish government awarded Scottish Aviation a contract to modify twelve MDAP ex-Royal Navy Douglas Skyraider early-warning aircraft for target towing duties - the Skyraider AEW-1. The aircraft were stored at RNAS Sanderling, Abbotsinch and taken by road at night for conversion at Prestwick. Twelve airframes were initially modified and included parts from other aircraft with the balance being scrapped. The radar was removed from the Skyraider and incorporated into the Fairey Gannet AEW3. Later the radar was once again removed from the Gannet and incorporated into the Avro Shackleton AEW aeroplane. The work, done under Scottish Aviation's SALchek service, involved removal from each aircraft the radar scanner, radome and associated equipment, the auxiliary fins, arrester hook and fixed slats and spoiler. The main instrument panel was redesigned and a winch operator's cabin was incorporated in the rear fuselage: this cabin includes seating for two, an auxiliary instrument panel and blister windows. Provision had also been made for the installation of the winch itself. A number of other installations

Spring 1963 WT966 at Prestwick

Skyraider target tug and electronic warfare SE-EBG in Sweden

SE-EBC wings folded in Sweden

had been designed and fitted to the aircraft. These include a civil radio station equipped with a King KX. 130 YHF/YOR/ILS system, Motorola ADF type T.12. TR.1934 VHF and a King KR.20 marker beacon receiver, together with an APN/1 radio altimeter. The completed aircraft were finished bright yellow overall. The first of the converted Skyraiders was flown to Sweden on 14 September 1962, following receipt of a Swedish Certificate of Airworthiness and six had been delivered by the beginning of March 1963. A further two were added to the total making fourteen in all. In addition to target towing four were utilised for electronic warfare and electronic intelligence gathering. They were operated by a private company, Svensk Flygtjanst AB, on behalf of the Swedish government.

AD-1 Skyraider

The initial single seat version of the Skyraider was powered by a 2,500 hp Wright R-3350-24W engine. Its details were as follows:

Weight empty 10,508 lbs
Gross (Scout) 13,924 lbs
Gross (Bomber) 18,030 lbs
Dimensions:
Wing span 50 ft
Length 38 ft 4 in
Height 17 ft 6 in
Ordnance on Fuselage:
Bombs one 2,000 lbs
Depth bomb one 650 lbs

Mine one 2,000 lbs
Torpedo one MK 13-3
Ordnance on Wings:
Bombs two 2,000 lbs
Depth Bombs two 650 lbs
Mines two 1,000 lbs
Rockets two 11.75 in. Tiny Tim
Twelve HVAR
Torpedo two MK 13-3
Guns: two 20mm Cannon (M3)

5

Media

Little Dieter needs to Fly - Director/Narrator - Werner Herzog,
Producer - Andre Singer, Screenwriter - Werner Herzog
Released in the United States 2 October 1998
Running time: 1 Hour 20 minutes Sound Mix Stereo
Dengler was taken prisoner of war by the Pathet Lao and then
turned over to soldiers of the Army of North Vietnam. After a
period of torture and starvation spent handcuffed to six other
prisoners in a bamboo prisoner-of-war camp, Dengler escaped. He
was subsequently rescued after being spotted by United States Air
Force pilot Eugene Deatrick. In the film Dieter Dengler is seen
having dinner with Eugene Deatrick. The bulk of the middle of the
film consists of footage from a trip Herzog took with Dengler back
to Laos and Thailand. To recreate his ordeal three decades after the
fact. Herzog hired locals to play the part of the captors and had
Dengler retrace his steps while describing his experiences. The
film is remarkable because of the way Dengler detaches from his
ordeal. As with all his work Herzog himself is never far from
proceedings, partly as interlocutor, partly as illustrator. It is a
fascinating story and one that has been done justice to. A postscript
consisting of footage from Dengler's funeral in 2001 was later
added to the film. Herzog subsequently directed Rescue Dawn, a
feature film based on the events of Dengler's capture,
imprisonment, escape, and rescue. That film, starring Christian
Bale as Dengler, was released on 24 July 2007.
Little Dieter Needs to Fly received critical acclaim on its release.

Awards

1997: Special Jury Award - International Documentary Film
     Festival Amsterdam
1998: IDA Award - International Documentary Association
1999: Gold Apple - National Educational Media Network,

USA
1999: Golden Spire - San Francisco International Film
   Festival
1999: Silver FIPA - Biarritz International Festival of
   Audio-visual Programming

Rescue Dawn

Rescue Dawn is a 2006 epic war drama film written and
directed by Werner Herzog, based on an adapted screenplay
written from his 1997 documentary film "Little Dieter Needs to
Fly." The film stars Christian Bale and is based on the true story
of German-American pilot Dieter Dengler, who was shot down
and captured by villagers sympathetic to the Pathet Lao during
an American military campaign in the Vietnam War. Steve
Zahn, Jeremy Davies, Pat Healy, and Toby Huss also have
principal roles. The film project, which had initially come
together during 2004, began shooting in Thailand in August
2005. It received critical acclaim but was a box office failure.

Filming

Principal photography took place over 44 days in Thailand. In
preparation for the roles, the actors playing the prisoners spent
several months losing weight. Since weight gain is
accomplished more quickly than weight loss, the film was shot
in reverse, with Bale fully regaining his weight during the
course of the shoot. The film includes the first major use of
digital visual effects in Herzog's career; the shots of Dengler's
flight while airborne were created digitally. The crash itself,
however, is live action.

Music and soundtrack

The original motion picture soundtrack for Rescue Dawn was released by the Milan Records label on 26 June 2007. It features classical music, with considerable use of the cello and piano. The score for the film was orchestrated by Klaus Badelt. Original songs written by musical artists Ernst Reijseger, Patty Hill, Craig Eastman, and Jack Shaindlin among others, were used in between dialogue shots throughout the film. Peter Austin edited the music.

Reception

Rescue Dawn was distributed by Metro-Goldwyn-Mayer theatrically in the United States, and by Pathe Distribution, Hopscotch Films and Central Film GmbH in foreign markets. It was originally scheduled to be released by MGM in December 2006, but was held back for limited release in the United States until 2007, with the full release on 27 July 2007 following a limited release in New York City, Toronto and Los Angeles on 4 July.

Critical response

Preceding its theatrical run, Rescue Dawn was generally met with positive critical reviews before its initial screening in cinemas. Among mainstream critics in the United States, the film received almost exclusively positive reviews. As of June 2020, the film holds a 90% approval rating on Rotten Tomatoes, based on 163 sampled critics review gave the film a positive review, with an average score of 7.52 out of 10.

Accolades

Following its cinematic release in 2007, Rescue Dawn was nominated for multiple awards, including a Golden Satellite

Award and an Independent Spirit Award. Among other nominations, Rescue Dawn was considered for the Golden Satellite Awards in the categories of "Best Supporting Male", "Best Supporting Actor" and "Best Actor in a Drama". The film garnered a win for actor Christian Bale from the San Diego Film Critics Society in the category of "Body of Work".

Literature

ESCAPE FROM LAOS By Dieter Dengler. San Rafael, Calif.: Presidio Press 211 pages, maps, one illustration. 1979/1996

VIETNAM AIR LOSSES by Chris Hobson, Midland Counties Publication, Hinckley, 2001

HERO FOUND by Bruce Henderson, Harper, New York, 2011

THE MILITARY AND THE MEDIA, 1962-1968, The U.S. Army in Vietnam, William M. Hammond, Centre of Military History, Washington, 1990

EASTWARD, A History of the Royal Air Force in the Far East 1945-1972, Air Chief Marshal Sir David Lee, GBE, CB, HMSO, London, 1984

Periodicals

Soldier of Fortune: February 1980 Page 27-29
Air Pictorial 1991
Stern Magazine, 14 August 1966, West Germany, translated
Central Intelligence Agency - Library of Congress
Evasion and Survival Case Study I escaped from a Red Prison by Dieter Dengler, in 17 pages, Library of Congress
FOLLOWING ARE HIGHLIGHTS DENGLER DEBRIEF, PWMASTER 120194 Library of Congress 1966
"COPTER MEN TELL OF RESCUE OF PILOT WHO

ESCAPED REDS" FROM THE EVENING STAR, July 28,
1966, Library of Congress
Imprisonment and escape of Lt (JG.) Dieter Dengler, USNR.
Hearing, Eighty-ninth Congress, second session ... September
16, 1966. Published/Created Washington, U.S. Govt. Print. Off.,
1966. Library of Congress

Sources

The Mitchell Library Pro-Quest, The Library of Congress, Trove.au,
United States National Archives, National Security Archives, Fold3,
Governmentattic.org etc.

Search Terms

Dieter Dengler, Skyraider, CVA-61 USS Ranger, EC-121, Jolly
Green Giant, 1st Air Commando, Da Nang, Dixie Station, Lieutenant
Eugene P. Deatrick, CIA.Gov-Reading Room

Aircraft Model Kits

Hobby Master 1:72 Air power Series HA2906
Douglas A-1J Skyraider Die-cast Model
USN VA-145 Swordsmen NK504 USS *Ranger* Vietnam 1966
(Discontinued)

Revell 1:40 Douglas Skyraider 1959-1994,(see page 43)
H269-198, H260-298, 0261, H-260-398, Sandy H-260, H-261,
8615, 0261 (Discontinued).